The Self-Renewing School

Part I
Design

Presents a design to transform a school system into an "academy," in which everyone is involved in action research on school improvement.

Presents the thesis that the interests of educators as learners and children as learners are intertwined. The process of renewal stimulates the faculty as it enhances the environment of the students.

Describes the teacher as individual, the school faculties, and the "central office" as interlocking spheres of the organization whose borders need to blur.

Describes the evolution of research and thought from the formulation of "inservice education" through the development of staff development systems to the centrality of school improvement and the need for the redevelopment of the culture of educators and the creation of self-renewing organizations.

Presents a set of principles, derived from research and experience, on which to generate the self-renewing organization.

Describes a strategy for redeveloping the system by reshaping initiatives for school improvement, creating a cadre, organizing leadership teams, and involving individuals and faculties in study groups.

Part II
Making It Happen

Presents a scenario in which the restructuring committee of a district consider the overall purposes of education and survey the literature on change and curricular and instructional options while gradually organizing the district faculty to create a self-renewing organization.

Describes the results of the restructuring committee's survey of research on school renewal, with special emphasis on efforts that have succeeded and some that have not.

Our policymakers survey several of the "common-sense" programs currently being employed or advocated and come up with some surprising findings.

Using the concept of "effect size," our district policymakers organize the entire district faculty into study groups who attack the literature on teaching strategies; curricular initiatives; and several large-scale, successful school improvement efforts.

Our district has prepared for their effort. The hard work is now to be done. The client has to be involved. What do we know that can help build a partnership with the community?

Discusses the cultural purposes of education that apply to all schools in the society. Identifies a series of current needs that should be addressed by contemporary educational systems.

Foreword

SCHOOLS, BEING THE WELL-ESTABLISHED SOCIAL INSTITUTIONS that they are, affect everyone's life. So it's not surprising that everyone, from the average citizen to the highest ranking government official, gives educators advice on ways to "fix" education. We recognize that these suggestions are well intentioned and in many instances quite appropriate. However, we know that to renew our schools, there is no quick fix and no single right answer to the problems that plague us. To do the job requires knowledge based on research and a collective effort by all stakeholders.

In *The Self-Renewing School*, the authors provide a research-based, practical guide for renewal that keeps one goal central: *improving student learning*. The process can be undertaken by a local school or an entire school district that is seriously interested in restructuring. It takes into account the importance of involving not only the central office staff, school administrators, teachers, and students, but also support personnel and the community at large. The authors caution us about those "detractors" or impediments to progress in achieving true educational reform: demanding change without adequately planning for implementation and staff development, tolerating fragmented approaches to curricular and instructional innovations, and engaging "strong leadership" that manipulates rather than collaborates.

Through scenarios describing the actions of a district restructuring committee, the book shows how the "interlocking spheres of the organization" cooperate, with roles and functions blending in leadership teams and study groups. Action research becomes the driving force in the evolution of such a self-renewing organization, and schools and districts choose reform initiatives with proven track records—and then support these efforts with carefully planned staff development.

Educational leaders preparing for school renewal should examine ways of implementing the four dimensions of innovation presented in this book: (1) content or substance, (2) procedures for mobilizing energy and providing support, (3) staff development, and (4) cultural change. All four dimensions recognize the centrality of student learning in any successful restructuring effort.

This book is timely in its discussion of school-based management, literacy, mastery learning, magnet schools, at-risk students, interdisciplinary studies, parent involvement, curriculum standards and frameworks, and technology. All these educational issues are examined through the lens of "effect size." In an analysis of research on student learning, which initiatives have produced the largest positive effects on student learning? Which ones have minimal effects? In the self-renewing school, study groups examine the literature and their own experiences to find initiatives with large effect sizes. And then all concerned, with "stubborn resolve to perfect our society and provide a better life for our children," work for change, including the entire community in the process.

Finally, the authors stress the urgency of implementing those practices and principles that provide the power for renewal if we are to be an educationally prepared nation for the 21st century. The book points us in the right direction.

BARBARA TALBERT JACKSON
ASCD President, 1993–94

Prologue

Grace, Fluidity, and Energy

Can we create a new generation of educational organizations?

Can we build on the best we have known and transform it productively? Can we move from the artificial distinctions between role designations of "teachers" and "administrators," of "school" and "central office" personnel? Can we build a situation where graceful interactions among all of us release the energy to build a new era of education? Can we reach beyond the limitations of our old conceptions of curriculum and teaching and organization to envision a fluid, powerful academy where teachers, community members, and students seek to grow: a place where the quest of the elders is the inspiration of the young, and the fresh promise of the young gives renewed life to the elders?

The Yellow Brick Road

If we think we can do it, then we can.

The wonderful message of *The Wizard of Oz* was that dreams are real. We actually have them. The little girl was right. And the wizard was a genial con. The child represents the richness and gaiety of a world of possibilities, and the wizard represents our self-imposed limitations.

The real secret to the development of a self-renewing world is that there is no secret. Our only enemies are our own fears and self-deceptions. Giving up these comfortable enemies allows us to see the levels of truth of which we are capable and the images we can conjure. And those levels and images are not so bad.

The core of the messages from research on change is that those who believe that a life worth living is worth living well do some pretty remarkable things. The search for safe and easy plans for "restructuring" generates the false gods, for such "easy" plans are built on the hope that we can discover a way of improving schools that simply rearranges the old elements—ourselves and our colleagues—in some way that magically increases the energy of the organization. In fact, the energy needed is that of human beings, and the major impediments we have to face are the ones we impose on ourselves. Relaxing into productive change is the key, rather than stiffening and bracing ourselves against the winds of change and hoping that our role in the new era will be just a freshly painted version of our current, familiar role.

The major theme in the current literature on change is actually quite simple and, once perceived, obvious: *Caring for children and caring for oneself and one's colleagues are one and the same.* We are talking about life here. The literature is full of examples of teachers enabling students, even the most unlikely ones, to learn to outstanding degrees and reach beyond prediction to a self-confident, socially committed state of growth. They and their teachers were enhanced. Love of self and others merged.

The self-renewing organization is different from others in many subtle ways, not in one big structural configuration. But all those little departures from ordinary interactions are connected to a really big idea—that human life is too important to be neglected in any way—and that the will to create a vital setting can overcome the obstacles that appear so large at times, but really are not *that* important, given the stakes.

This book is the product of reflection on several thousand studies of teaching strategies, curriculum designs, site-centered school improvement efforts, action research projects, staff development designs, and the general literature on innovation, school renewal, and the culture of the school. The citations throughout are illustrative and range from reflective reports and specific studies to summaries of research on particular areas. The citations in Part II represent what the authors believe will be discovered if a group of policymakers conduct the kind of inquiry described in this book.

BRUCE JOYCE
JAMES WOLF
EMILY CALHOUN

PART I

DESIGN

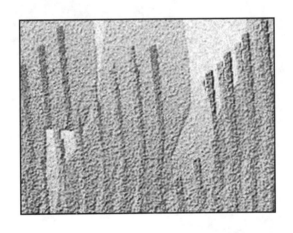

1 The Self-Renewing Organization

THIS BOOK IS ABOUT THE ORGANIZATION THAT WE CALL THE school district. By *district* we do not mean the "central office" or the board of education. We mean the entire organization of teachers; school administrators; curricular, instructional, and technological support personnel; and participating citizens. The issue we address is how to sort out research on organizational culture and innovation, blend it with experience in school improvement, and generate a design for an organization that is self-renewing.

In the self-renewing organization, educators in all positions in the system create a better learning environment for themselves and students by studying education and how to improve it. The resulting initiatives for educational improvement propel the students into more active states of learning; and the greater activity of the students, in turn, stimulates the educators to engage in more study and create even more vigorous learning environments. An enriching spiral is generated.

In Part I, we present a rationale and design for the self-renewing organization. We have tried to build on the best features of the school district as we know it (there are many good features), use research where we could find it (there is a lot of research), and fill in the blanks with our collective experience and ideas we scrounged from our colleagues. In Part II, we deal with first steps for changing the organization in the form of a scenario in which the restructuring committee of a school district examine the research on change and

---

Authors' Note: Our formulation owes more than a little to the spirit of the arguments advanced a few years ago by John Gardner (e.g., Gardner 1963, 1987), some of which influenced Waterman's (1988) *The Renewal Factor.*

on alternative initiatives in curriculum and instruction and prepare their district for action.

The quality of schooling and the work lives of educators are inextricably entwined. Educators and the public acknowledge that both need dramatic improvement. Consequently, recommendations and initiatives for school improvement abound, both broad (Goodlad 1984, Sizer 1984, Bloom 1984, Eisner 1991) and narrow; but school organizations have not been fertile ground for innovations suggested from either within or without (Cuban 1990; Sarason 1982, 1990; Adler 1982; Fullan and Miles 1991; Miles 1992). Whether teachers, principals, district or state personnel, or research teams have been the source, proposals for curricular, instructional, or technological improvements have struggled and, in too many cases, gone by the wayside (Fullan and Pomfret 1977, Sarason 1990, David and Peterson 1984, Goodlad and Klein 1970, Miles and Huberman 1984). Moreover, proposals for school improvement have often created enough internal strife that innovation is generally regarded as a hazardous business (Huberman 1992).

Teachers and observers of schools have increasingly complained about the sterility and stress of the school as a workplace where new ideas are so often stillborn. Yet most people in education, while feeling that it is very difficult to make significant changes, have the simultaneous impression that they live in the midst of a torrent of "mandates" for change. Both feelings are correct. In most schools and districts, dozens of half-implemented innovations and "pilot" programs operate at any one time, but thoroughgoing or pervasive changes are rare. Teachers have been virtually shell-shocked by barrages of "semi-changes" that sap energy while making few substantial differences. Yes, innovation is harrowing work because organizational shortcomings have made the work setting of educators a difficult one for the deep exercise of fresh ideas on a widespread basis, while the sounds of imminent change are almost deafening.

In an odd sense, the act of innovation is itself an innovation when an organization is not self-renewing. Because educational organizations are designed to be stable rather than dynamic, even the simplest substantive change requires that the innovators, whatever their official roles, have to deal not only with the innovation itself, but create conditions that will sustain the innovation, which can disappear quickly if the context is not maintained. Thus our claim: The self-renewing organization will be better for everyone because all members will be in an accelerated and richer state of growth, working together for school improvement, rather than making the school a "social battleground," to use Charlotte Sudderth's (1989) felicitous words. Collective inquiry concerning the effects of our actions on students—learning with and from each other and gaining in knowledge, technical skills, and interpersonal relations—sustains school renewal. In this healthier environment, promising changes can be made as an ordinary part of organizational life, rather than being thrust into uncongenial territory.

In addition to learning new things, to create this healthy, growth-producing culture, we may have to let go of some practices and ideas that have hitherto seemed reasonable, even dear, to us. Perhaps the most important changes are attitudinal—acknowledging that our organization needs more than a little fixing, and affirming that educators are up to the job of changing it radically. With respect to the first attitude, most of us have operated on the assumption that the way America conducts education has been basically sound, if a little flawed and out-of-date, and that mild changes will take care of things. The need for strong change has not been embraced generally. One reason the need for change has not been more robustly central is the tacit notion that change is not necessary unless the current state can be proved to be terrible. What we have often ignored in our restructuring efforts is that (1) the chief reason for seeking improvement is that the search enlivens the organization for adults and students alike and (2) improvement is possible regardless of the current state of the organization. In other words, the best can always get better. We do not have to begin by asserting that the current state is dreadful.

The affirmation that educators *can* change the organization is also important, because another reason that initiatives have not been made stronger is concern that personnel could make only mild changes at best, either in instruction or in the nature of the workplace (Sarason 1991). Some past initiatives were related directly to opportunities for student learning (such as curricular and instructional changes and use of the computer); some promoted collegial relationships among faculty (such as "site-based" management). Many such initiatives have been designed to edge gradually into their target area so as not to disturb what were perceived to be the fragile sensibilities of the personnel.

Partially because of this social and cognitive "kid gloves" approach to change, an implicit policy of gradualism has taken shape. Initiatives have frequently been so tentative that they have disappeared in the implementation (Goodlad and Klein 1970; Cuban 1990; Huberman and Miles 1984, 1986). A nasty side effect has been the cynicism that has developed among the public and among teachers. By making demands for change without adequate planning for implementation, central offices and trustees have discredited their legitimacy in the eyes of many teachers who currently reject initiatives from their appointed leaders because they have evidence that inadequate support will be given to them (Huberman 1992). In fact, strong, well-supported initiatives are easier to make than are weak ones; and *educators are perfectly capable of rapidly learning the skills and knowledge to sustain the most complex initiatives thus far put forward, provided that adequate support is given.* In many cases, very great changes have been made—as in the cases of the Success for All program (Madden, Slavin, Karweit, Dolan, and Wasik 1991, 1993) and the Richmond County, Georgia, School Improvement Program (Joyce, Murphy, Showers, and Murphy 1989)—because entire organizations (i.e., school districts and their schools) acknowledged the complexity of the change and provided the technical and social support necessary to make things work. The "site-based" school improvement and action research movements include both cases where schools became "stuck" (David and Peterson 1984) and cases where outstanding school teams were able to transform the social organization of the school and bring about significant changes in one to three years (Calhoun 1992, Glickman 1993). The majority of schools have been "stuck" because, we believe, the effort was too tentative to move the organization. The "toe-in-the-water" approach underestimates what people can do and what the organization needs.

Although established attitudes and ideas need to give way to new ones in many other areas (we discuss several of these areas later in this book), the organizational acknowledgement of the need for major changes in schooling and this affirmation of collective efficacy are critical. Anyone who believes that "We're okay, Jack," or that educators cannot stand the stress of change will quickly give up the quest for serious school improvement. As we struggle to initiate school renewal that sustains healthy learning communities, educators should take comfort from the fact that we *can* change the whole organization and how it does business—and we can do so quite rapidly. We contend that the major problem has not been the personnel (we reject the notion that educators are inherently loathe to risk taking), but is found in the nature and design of the organization. As we change the organization, the creativity and vitality of both educators and students will be enhanced immeasurably.

> Happiness is neither virtue nor pleasure nor this thing nor that but simply growth. We are happy when we are growing.
>
> William Butler Yeats

2 Redefining the District as Academy: A Proposal

THE REDEFINED SCHOOL ORGANIZATION BECOMES A LEARNING center for everyone. We call it an *academy*, a community of colleagues gathered to study and advance knowledge. Some of our colleagues are children, who, although our clients, are collaborators in learning. Some of us, the older, take special responsibility for groups of the younger folks, but no more than they do, as they mature, for themselves. Some of us coordinate things. Some are given more time than others to worry about the health of the system, and everyone accepts the responsibility for supporting the total learning community. We concentrate in this book on the dimension by which *the adults renew themselves in the service of improving the education of the young*. The time is right to build a setting in which the study of our craft enlarges the education of everyone in the organization, whether they are four or seventy-four.

The argument that the time has come to focus on self-renewing capacities is bolstered by a combination of developments. Research from the fields of change, innovation, and school improvement has advanced significantly (Fullan with Steigelbauer 1991, Madden et al. 1993, Huberman and Miles 1984, Hopkins 1990). A considerable evolution in research and thought on staff development has changed conceptions of its purposes and how to conduct it (Joyce and Showers 1988; Joyce, ed., 1990). Research on instruction continues to progress and has productively explored new avenues (Johnson and Johnson 1989; Dole, Duffy, Roehler, and Pearson 1991; Pressley, Levin, and Delaney 1982). New research is available on how the culture of organizations affects the ability to effect change (Hopkins 1992, Fullan with Steigelbauer 1991). The catastrophic effects of some highly touted initiatives, such as magnet schools (Moore and

Davenport 1989), and the indifferent effects of some site-based management initiatives (David and Peterson 1984, Louis and Miles 1990) have raised an extensive series of questions. We need to find out why such popular and seemingly correct avenues have been unsuccessful in many places; whereas some inexpensive and relatively easy-to-implement initiatives, such as using research-based teaching strategies (Johnson and Johnson 1989, Sharan and Shachar 1988), have shown dramatic benefits for students when well implemented. In other words, things have not always turned out as expected: some of the most commonly used strategies for school renewal have had negative side effects, while some of the less obvious avenues have been working well (Joyce and Calhoun 1991).

There are those who say we are more likely to repeat the mistakes of the past in our current efforts to improve education (Bennis 1989, Cuban 1990, Sarason 1990), but we won't do that. We will use our cumulative knowledge simultaneously with our individual and collective reflections to create a new generation of educational organizations—one far more healthy for all of us.

Interdependence in a Self-Renewing System

Generating new levels of interdependence is extremely important. School districts are composed of three organizational structures, or spheres. The largest sphere includes *individual teachers*. They work as *faculties in schools* (the second sphere) and are related to support and coordinating personnel from what is usually called the *district office* (the third sphere). For continuity, we refer to these structures or spheres by their familiar names: the *teacher*, the *school*, and the *district office*, although we later propose changes in the relationships among them.

These three socioprofessional spheres hold joint responsibility for educating all students within the organization. Although myriad individual purposes and levels of energy exist within each sphere, in the self-renewing organization they are different chiefly in terms of size. Their primary goals and functions are the same—to build the learning environment that nurtures the growth of everyone who touches the academy. In our current educational organization, the spheres have often drifted apart and worked at odds with each other.

In some cases, the language and structure of the "worker" and "manager" have dominated; in others, relationships and responsibilities have so fragmented across the spheres that adversarial relationships, evidenced by lack of trust and heavy regulation, dominate the district.

To counter this fragmentation and to promote unity, we plan our workplace activities differently. In a self-renewing organization—the academy—we use all we know about instruction, social learning theory, and adult development to plan these collective work times. We design our workplace interactions so that individuals within and across each sphere and the groups that compose each sphere work together to become scholars of their work and to stimulate and support one another. As a signal to remind us of our cognitive and social interdependence, we use somewhat different terms for the roles within each sphere:

• Individual scholar-teachers who study teaching, curriculum, and academic and social content

• Faculties as communities of scholar-professionals engaged in school improvement, simultaneously enhancing the quality of their life and the quality of education of children

• District office personnel as scholar-coordinators who tend the quality of the community by their own study and by facilitating the study and generation of initiatives to improve curriculum, instruction, and technology

Within the organization, an evolving cadre of scholars, drawn from all role groups and spheres, provide service and leadership to their colleagues on content ranging from the development of problem-solving communities to issues of curriculum, instruction, and technology. Thus, initiatives are not generated and passed down through a hierarchy, but are formulated by individual scholar-teachers and faculties under a canopy of technical and social support woven by the cadre and designed to enhance learning for all members of the organization, including themselves as cadre members. The formation of this holistic learning community promotes the interdependence that is necessary for collective growth in the midst of widely divergent individual needs.

A Change in Cultural Patterns and Roles

Developing a self-renewing capability changes the culture of educators and the ways they approach their roles and relate to one another and to the organization as a structure for their work. Teachers become reflective practitioners who continually expand their repertoire of tools and study the effects of these strategies on students. Teachers operate in study groups and as faculties who work together to implement new teaching strategies and curriculums. Scholar-teachers and scholar-principals are skilled in action research for school improvement and in ways of organizing and supporting change (Glickman 1990). Principals coordinate leadership teams composed of teachers and parents. District curriculum and instruction personnel facilitate school initiatives and interface with schools to ensure the implementation of curriculum improvements and to support the study of teaching. District office personnel coordinate systemwide initiatives in technology and curriculum development and help design and provide the resources and staff development necessary to implement these curricular and technological changes. In time, all personnel come to understand how individuals and organizations change and innovate, what relationships exist among the spheres of the organization, and how to collaborate to bring about educational improvement.

Thus, the activities of the organization are not characterized as "top down" or "bottom up," because enterprises from all spheres and levels are legitimized. The system is one of "co-leadership." (Fullan and Miles 1991 use the term *co-management*.) Communication throughout the organization is continuous, and "vertical" and "horizontal" distinctions are changed. People within all three spheres carefully coordinate ideas and actions, giving consideration to the energy and needs of different people across the organization and to the content and requirements of the initiatives. Co-leaders integrate changes in curriculum, instruction, and technology and stage these changes to prevent overload. Co-leaders assign priorities to innovations and vigorously support those that are initiated. Co-leaders carefully induct new personnel into the organization and into their roles as collaborators in school improvement.

The organizational structure and operations that we propose are constructed on a set of principles developed from our analysis of the literature and reflection on our experiences with innovations in education. We are encouraged that the experience with some seemingly quite different approaches to school improvement appear to be generating some of the same ideas both about the educational system and about how it can become self-renewing. Among the three coauthors of this book, one has extensive experience with both action research and innovation in language instruction. Another has broad experience with innovations in curriculum and instruction and staff development. Another has presided over major changes in the development of collegial organizations throughout a school district, the implementation of a wide range of innovations, and the development of a core of lead teachers and principals who can build collegial organizations. We have all learned many of the same things, although our roles have been very different, as have been the substances of our innovations. Most important, *all three of us have reported substantial gains in student achievement* following such initiatives. Our experience coincides with the recent research on change and the recommendations of others who have experience with complex innovations.

⁊   ⁊   ⁊

The principles we now turn to and the ways of thinking about the dimensions of the organization will, individually, all seem familiar to the student of organizational development. None, by itself, is radical. But taken together, these principles become the basis for making a significant difference in the texture of the organization.

3 How Research and Experience Shaped the Principles of Self-Renewal

THE SCHOOL RENEWAL LITERATURE OF THE PAST TWENTY-FIVE years shows a steady progression of ideas for improving education. Two areas provide illuminating examples of the progression: staff development, on which so many aspects of school renewal depend, and the study of implementation and change.

Linear, "Top-Down" Staff Development

During the 1960s and much of the 1970s, districts generated most staff development to implement curriculum changes, largely through workshops, and a linear model of change was in vogue. (People at the "top" designed curriculum, provided training, and expected implementation.) During those years, however, workshops were brief or separated from the workplace, as in the case of the National Science Foundation Institutes that carried the Academic Reform Movement from the 1950s to the 1970s. Little in-school follow-up was provided. In most districts, schools implemented little change beyond the periodic exchange of older textbooks for newer ones (Fullan and Pomfret 1977). Many states and regions established a large network of development centers and laboratories; but despite their efforts, a series of highly publicized and often heavily funded curriculum reforms had very little impact on curriculum and instruction (Goodlad and Klein 1970). The provision of service to schools and teachers had simply been too weak to sustain innovations, even those that were well researched, were properly implemented, and had substantial effects on student learning. Some of the reforms in mathematics and science education (Bredderman 1983, El Nemr 1979), for example, improved student learning dramatically both in content and degree when thoroughly supported, but were not effectively realized in most school settings.

The focus shifted toward providing more elaborate support in schools and districts; and the term *staff development* came into common use by the mid-1970s. The scope of content offered through workshops and institutes widened greatly during the 1980s, and leaders added varieties of teaching skills and models of teaching. Although a "field" of staff development emerged, most workshops continued to be relatively short, with little follow-up; and evaluation indicated poor levels of implementation of the content. Also, these workshops often presented teaching skills in isolation from curriculum content; workshop examples resembled a collection of puzzle pieces that the participants were left to integrate on their own.

When educators recognized the ineffectiveness of the fragmentary approaches, researchers shifted their attention to training and staff development, leadership, and the characteristics of schools that appeared to be more or less congenial to change. It was important to acknowledge that there was a problem, because many educators had *believed* that they could "manage change," when in fact most could not. This acknowledgment licensed the research teams to dig deeper than they had before and try to generate guidelines for improved practice.

Research-Based Procedures

In the mid-1970s and early 1980s, research on staff development entered a highly productive time. *Educators created procedures that could ensure substantial degrees of implementation of curricular and instructional innovations*, at least on a temporary basis, and these procedures were often accompanied by *substantial improvement in student learning* (Johnson and Johnson 1990; Joyce, Murphy, Showers, and Murphy 1989; Joyce and Showers 1988; Sharan and Shachar 1988; Slavin 1990; Walberg 1990; Cochran-Smith 1991; Bloom 1984; Becker 1977). A technology for helping people to learn and implement new skills was emerging. Educators came to see the product of staff development as innovations (for the participants) in curriculum and instruction. *Essentially, if the content is worthwhile, it is new; and new content, if implemented, is an innovation.* Simultaneously, as the technology developed and it became clear that staff development was in the innovation business, *it also became clear from scholarship on change that innovation is a constantly evolving, multidimensional process rather than a mechanical, linear sequence of events* (Elmore 1990, 1992; Fullan 1990; Fullan and Steigelbauer 1991; Lieberman 1988; Baldridge and Deal 1983; Leithwood 1990; Hallinger and McCary 1991).

No simple formula will emerge for implementing healthy staff development systems (or for creating self-renewing organizations). Our initiatives will have to proceed with the acknowledgment that much more knowledge will have to come out of those efforts. Also, as studies of leadership have evolved, we are beginning to recognize that effective leaders are effective problem solvers and community builders. Thus we have shifted our emphasis in staff development from a search for formulas of skills toward an attempt to understand how effective problem-solvers function (Hallinger and McCary 1991).

"Rolling" Models of Change

As the 1990s proceed, the success of the research on staff development—together with published reflections on field experience—has led to a more complex view of the change process (Fullan, Bennett, and Rolheiser-Bennett 1990; Huberman 1992; Leithwood 1990; Hallinger and McCary 1991; Levine 1991; Showers 1989; Baker 1983; Joyce and Showers 1988; Joyce 1992), especially a movement from linear to "rolling" models of change (Huberman 1992). In addition, as we have developed more effective implementation procedures and studied their results, we have increasingly found that productive staff development is still an innovation in itself (Fullan 1990).

Because we have not fully solved the problem of implementing strong and responsive systems of staff development, our understanding of staff development as a dimension of school renewal is still evolving. Educators must acknowledge this level of complexity and squarely face it. Otherwise, energetic and dedicated people trying to improve the system will become discouraged because projects fail when they have not taken into account the full range of factors that need to be dealt with. Considering many dimensions of school renewal simultaneously may seem intimidating at first, but it is healthier to face the complexity than to risk failure because we have neglected important components. For example, asking teachers to engage in collective decision making without providing *time* for meetings can sabotage an otherwise well-designed effort.

The titles of yearbooks of major education organizations reflect the evolution of staff development in school renewal. The 1957 yearbook of the National Society for the Study of Education was *Inservice Education*. The 1981 ASCD yearbook was *Staff Development/Organizational Change*, and the 1990 ASCD yearbook was *Changing School Culture Through Staff Development*. "Inservice education" implied service to the staff of an essentially well-functioning organization. "Staff development and organizational change" implied a far stronger level of service that included changes in the organization. "Changing school culture through staff development" implies that the social arrangements of the organization have to change if school improvement is to be an embedded feature of the organization.

Our early concepts of innovation and inservice education included neither a very well-developed understanding of innovation nor a vision of the change process. Teachers and administrators would take courses and, with little help, incorporate any new content into their daily work. We now recognize that changes in curriculum and instruction are extremely complex—that changing behaviors and attitudes involves effort that requires much support and energy. Such support demands a social system that enables people to focus appropriate levels of energy on the change process. Moreover, school improvement involves collective, innovative action and constant assessment of this action. Some discomfort arises from the realization that we have to make far deeper changes than were previously thought. Recognizing this need for deep change is understandably uncomfortable—but also comforting. What is comforting is that the many failed efforts of the past do not have to be replicated. It will be easier to face the complexity of change than to try to manage low-probability ad hoc approaches.

The evolution of thought has considerable implications for practice and also illustrates how rapidly useful knowledge can be accumulated and used to free us from habitual and constraining behavior. For we are learning all the time! For example, the practices of the "leading" staff development and curriculum implementation programs of ten years ago are now recognized to be relatively ineffectual. There is no reason to continue them.

Dimensions of Change

Today, we perceive *four significant dimensions to a substantive innovation for school renewal*: substance in curriculum, instruction, or technology; mobilization for action and the development of common understandings; staff development that generates cognition *and* new modes of interaction among members of the organization; and cultural change:

1. The *dimension of content or substance* of innovations (curriculum, instruction, and technology) defines how the student's learning environment will be changed, including the models of learning that will be used.

2. The *dimension of procedures for mobilizing energy and providing support* creates the common understandings and the organizational moves necessary to generate collective activity and cooperative problem-solving.

3. The *dimension of staff development* describes the system for learning new curricular, instructional, technological, and organizational procedures.

4. The *dimension of cultural change* defines the social relationships and understandings that generate the self-renewing organization and allow the other dimensions to function in an appropriate social matrix.

Today, we face a double challenge. First, we must build comprehensive approaches to innovation that move away from the fragmented, single-initiative approaches (even well-designed ones). Second, we must elevate the content, processes, and social organization of staff development and school improvement so that all spheres of the organization are served in an integrated manner. Current major writers on staff development show remarkable agreement on this integrated approach, especially considering that many of these people come from very different specialties, including:

- Specialists in *organizational behavior* (Little 1982, Rosenholtz 1989, Bolam 1990, Hopkins 1992)
- Specialists in *leadership* (Baldridge and Deal 1983, Murphy 1990)
- Specialists in *change*, such as Miles, Louis, Huberman, and Crandall (see Crandall et al. 1982)
- Specialists in *training* (Joyce and Showers 1988), as well as generalists who study *staff development* (Loucks-Horsley, et al. 1987) and students of the *action research* process (Holly 1991, Calhoun 1992).

These researchers have contributed much to our vision of how to begin creating the self-renewing school and district. Principles synthesized from their work form both the basis for the organizational structure and the guidelines for its operation.

✾   ✾   ✾

Thus, no single study or line of work has generated any one of the principles we are about to describe. The literature is vast and represents a variety of styles of research. The new convergence of findings and thought that is occurring is giving us a grounded set of themes on which we can proceed with some confidence. The style of thought that is currently ascendant has a considerable history in the work of (1) the founders of the social psychology of organizations, such as Lewin (1948) and his associates, and (2) the creators of direct approaches to help persons in organizations study and improve their process and technology while carrying out their duties (Thelen 1954; Bradford, Gibb, and Benne 1964). These researchers have worked for decades to develop frameworks on which self-renewing organizations can be built.

4 Principles and Rationales of Self-Renewing Organizations

THE PRINCIPLES OF SELF-RENEWAL ARE MANIFESTED IN THREE areas: cognition, relationships, and the socioprofessional processes of educational change. In self-renewing schools, the mission encompasses all spheres of the organization—the teachers, the local school, and the district—and *the centrality of student learning is the driving purpose of all activities.*

Mission of the Self-Renewing School

We must keep student learning central for two reasons: First, it is the purpose of education; second, it is technically necessary for school renewal.

In all reported cases of school improvement initiatives in which substantial student learning occurred, school staff kept students' interests as learners central throughout the planning, implementation, and assessment phases. We did not find a single case in the literature where student learning increased but had not been a central goal. Thus, even though we may plan school improvement initiatives as a way to improve the organization or adult life in the workplace, we must always select the content and procedures of these initiatives because there is a reasonable probability that students will benefit from them. *Thus, collegiality among educators, from the perspective of benefits for students, is a means to an end.* Instructional initiatives (such as cooperative learning) are selected and implemented *because of their potential and their documented success for increasing stu-*

dents' social and cognitive abilities, and effects are measured in terms of student learning. As we discuss later in this chapter and in Chapter 5, an essential part of school improvement efforts is a thorough study of implementation—in the form of "action research." This research includes making predictions, based on prior research, about what effects on students can be expected with a given degree and level of use of, say, cooperative learning in the classroom.

Because even highly desirable change involves necessary degrees of stress and inner turbulence (Huberman 1992), a number of researchers (see summaries in Joyce and Showers 1988; Joyce, Showers, and Weil 1992) believe that *major school improvement efforts can be sustained only when the content promises student learning.* Otherwise, the changes in organizational behavior and the struggle for implementation are likely to be perceived as too stressful to be worthwhile.

Studies of schools engaged in "site-based" programs for the improvement of education indicate that many school faculties, even some in heavily funded programs such as the California School Improvement Program (SIP), have great difficulty making initiatives that involve curriculum implementation and instruction (David and Peterson 1984, Louis and Miles 1990, Calhoun 1992). Instead, these schools make minor improvements in faculty relations (changes in faculty meeting times or bus duty rosters), parent relations (times for conferences), and regulations for students (attendance policies). As a result, many of these schools do not focus on the content and process of education, where the greatest possibility for payoff resides. Essentially, the mission is lost unless learning remains at the core.

Even some large-scale general programs—such as magnet schools and "categorical" programs for limited-English-speaking students or "gifted and talented" students—have frequently bogged down in regulations. Moreover, many people have ignored evidence that some of these programs were not achieving their purposes or, worse, were having negative effects (as in the case of magnet schools; see Moore and Davenport 1989). The centrality of student learning becomes lost as the details of program implementation become ends in themselves.

School improvement programs that result in dramatic positive learning gains for students keep the mission up front at all times. A good example is the Success for All program (Madden et al. 1993), whose very title keeps the purpose visible and whose structure is directly aimed at the learning problems it seeks to remedy. "Mastery learning" (Bloom 1984) is another approach that keeps the purpose central, as does the Coalition for Essential Schools (Sizer 1991). As near as we can tell, all successful school improvement programs manage to keep the mission at the fore and build communities whose members navigate the anxieties of implementation by supporting one another as they keep their common purpose paramount.

Scholar-teachers and scholar-coordinators know that many fine curricular, instructional, and technological options exist—options well backed by research and evaluation (see Joyce and Showers 1988; Joyce, Showers, and Weil 1992; Walberg 1990; Madden et al. 1993; Bloom 1984). Research results from these options have demonstrated effects on student learning that were unthinkable even a few years ago. From a student-learning point of view, the choices we now make among these options are significant, and knowledge of these choices creates a moral demand for action. Part of professional life in a self-renewing school is informed choice among options and disciplined study of the effects of these choices on the lives of our students.

Cognition and Cultural Change

Cognition: An inquiry-oriented, action-research frame of reference pervades the operations.

In a self-renewing organization, initiatives for change in curriculum and instruction or the workplace are not ends in themselves. Participants continually study student learning and judge school-improvement initiatives by their effect on what students learn and whether students increase their capability as learners. School and district staff make only those curricular changes that are likely to increase student learning—and only if staff plan to carefully study the implementation and its effects. Self-renewing schools discontinue the practice of automatic changes through adoption of materials on "cycles." Rather, they change the aspects of a curriculum that promise increases in certain types of student achievement.

In self-renewing schools, initiatives in instruction become a series of avenues to school improvement and are treated as such, with the effects examined carefully and collectively. For example, scholar-teachers study cooperative learning, not because it is fashionable, but because they fully realize the effects to be expected when the strategy is accompanied by proper implementation and effectively designed staff development. Implementation and assessment of effects are integral parts of the initiative. A self-renewing school is inquiry oriented. School staff examine evidence before they adopt initiatives, and they examine evidence when changes are made. Teachers make adjustments as they assess the impact of changes. Life in the organization is conducted in an experimental mode. Thus, in a self-renewing school, everyone—individuals, small groups, faculties, the cadre, committees that cross spheres, and central office personnel—engages in action research on a continuous basis, keeping the central mission at the heart of the operation.

In traditionally conducted education, not only are people isolated by role and by sphere, but they work in an information-poor environment that makes it difficult or impossible to clarify problems, select initiatives, or determine effects. By engaging in collegial action research, the members clarify areas needing attention; select initiatives on the basis of the best available evidence; and, by tracking implementation, determine effects on students. Staff members then adjust initiatives or select new ones—and they create a new professional community.

As we keep student learning central to any efforts to make the organization of the school better, we should also consider the nature of a healthy organization and how to bring it about. *Thus, all personnel become students of school improvement. An integrated culture of professionals is developed.* Everyone becomes knowledgeable about:

- Group decision making
- Options for staff development
- Collegial implementation of curriculum
- Action research for school improvement
- Change as a personal and organizational process

Instead of something done to people, staff development becomes an activity that everyone helps develop—and everyone profits. Individuals and faculties use the relationship among the three spheres and capitalize on their dynamics to help each other reach goals. The organizational structure thus becomes nurturing.

Fullan's (1990) direct and sensible summary of the need for cultural change emphasizes that *everyone* in the educational system needs to study the nature of change, if schooling is to become congenial to innovation. The community of researchers who are trying to forge principles to guide school improvement has shown uncommon agreement that this study of change is necessary across role groups.

Fullan's guiding thesis—the development of a community where *everyone* becomes expert in knowledge about change—leads to large differences in thought about innovation. These new ideas have the potential to greatly affect how educators view their roles and their relationship to school improvement. Rather than concentrating on a few persons who manage or manipulate change, who motivate others to innovate, or who support innovation, the self-renewing school would encourage *all* personnel to study change and learn how to work together to improve education. *If the organization recreates itself into a healthy learning community where working together, studying together, and growing together has been planned into the system as a way of life, working in schools becomes synonymous with lifelong learning.*

Think how our workplace would feel if the following were to happen:

• All persons in the organization, regardless of title, seek individual growth as a professional, accept responsibility as a group member for the growth of colleagues, and design their work to achieve the collectively valued goals of the school or district.

• All personnel study the technical aspects of change: how to learn new teaching skills, to incorporate new technologies, to implement curriculums, and to cope with the stress that inevitably accompanies change.

In such a learning organization, the role dichotomies that have characterized educational systems would disappear. The abrasions that have separated roles—teachers from principals, faculties from district offices, and educators from lay boards and policymakers— would diminish as everyone studied the educational process and how to improve it. The shared understandings and the increased collective ability to study and change practice would transform the culture of schooling (Fullan and Miles 1991).

One of the most important findings from the study of the implementation of initiatives for change comes from the work of Hall, Loucks-Horsley, Hord, Fuller and their associates (e.g., Hall and Hord 1987). These researchers have concentrated on the progression from tentative exploration of an innovation to routine, mechanical use and beyond. Just as important, the researchers have described the emotional stages that personnel experience as they learn to use something new in the classroom. Their initial reaction to an innovation is "self-concern," when the practitioner becomes worried about her own skill and how the students will respond to a new procedure. Frequently, the anxiety generated at this stage becomes dominant; and, when it does, the teacher is likely to discard the innovation to relieve the anxiety.

What are other ways to relieve this anxiety? One method is to create social support groups, such as study-group/peer-coaching arrangements (Joyce and Showers 1988). The purpose of an innovation—to build a better learning environment for students—has to be central, or the study groups will not maintain their efforts. The traditional isolation of the classroom has worked against the support needed during the natural periods of anxiety that accompany complex learning. Another way to relieve the anxiety is to be honest about it in the classroom and make it an essential part of our professional mission—teaching students *how* to learn. We can take some comfort as we navigate our own anxieties because we are sending a powerful message to students: we are demonstrating our own continued growth as individual learners and as professionals.

Organizers and trainers (from either the school or the district) are not immune to innovation anxiety. As school-based practitioners express their concerns, transmit the pressures they are feeling, or complain about the changes they are trying to make, organizers of training or follow-up are very likely to become discouraged and even back off. *Too often, the original reason for the innovation becomes submerged in the emotional turbulence created in the early stages of practice. In these early stages, practitioners are learners. They may feel less competent as they experiment with new teaching strategies; yet they may fail to recognize that their insecurity and discomfort are natural.* In fact, unless social support is created, self-concern often becomes so great that new practices are never tried (Joyce and Showers 1988). As organizers back off (they, too, are learners), the original idea becomes one of those things that "seemed like a good idea at the time," but that could not quite be carried off or just "was not practical."

Building our self-renewing organization requires that we learn how to think differently, and thinking differently will change us more than will the new, visible changes in our behavior.

Collaboration and Professionalization

The self-renewing school or district provides colleagueship directly within and across all spheres. Reflective teachers (Schön 1982) connected to reflective faculties (Schaefer 1967) connected to district councils (Joyce 1977), all supported by the cadre, eliminate the isolation inherent in the present organizational structure while respecting individual differences. The organization thus becomes a "center of inquiry" (Schaefer 1967), where the study of student learning is at the core of professional interchange. We design our action plans for studying, implementing, and assessing initiatives to use the benefits of the collaborative workplace to accomplish our goals and to improve the health of the organization. *We create a more effective organization and a healthier place to live and work at the same time.*

The norms of isolation and extreme autonomy that have characterized schooling (Lortie 1975, Little 1990, Rosenholtz 1989), the friction and confusion between levels of the organization, and the fragmentation of initiatives are increasingly understood as unhealthy. As difficult as it is technically, research is gradually establishing a clear connection between the mental health of the organization and the people in it and the growth of students (Mortimore, Sammons, Stoll, Lewis, and Ecob 1988; Argyris and Schön 1974; Houle 1980; Brookover 1978). Even were there no clear evidence, the relationship would be obvious. Integrated organizations, with collaborative social climates, are more healthy to work in and generate more job satisfaction across roles (Herzberg 1968). Inefficient and scattered staff development frustrates everyone. The excessive isolation of teachers and administrators is dangerous to our health. People involved in large-scale attempts to help schools—such as Levine and Lezotte (1990), who help schools use the mirror of the research on effective schools to generate activity, and Sizer (1991), who uses a model of academic excellence for the same purpose—all comment that one of the major problems encountered initially is the history of isolation as opposed to collegial inquiry. Even highly structured approaches to school improvement, such as Distar (Becker 1977), have had to expend disproportionately large amounts of energy on social organization, even though they rely on technology for their designs.

When all spheres of the organization are able to generate and implement initiatives, the sense of efficacy of each member and each faculty should increase substantially. Cadre members play a major "demonstration" role to help us learn this new way of living together. As they provide assistance to personnel and make the provision of information and clear communication part of their mission, they model the colleagueship and trust necessary to enable within- and across-sphere collaboration for school improvement.

Integration of the Spheres Within the Organization

The three spheres of the organization—the teacher, the school, and the district—are responsible for improving instruction and supporting one another. The self-renewing organization is integrated, and its work is integrative.

Thus, the idea that curriculum can be "controlled" by district office personnel is given up, as are the notions that school improvement is solely "site based" and that teachers as individuals are the ultimate decision makers regarding innovation. All of these positions have been more common in the literature than has the idea of an integrated organization. Many change efforts have been oriented to bridge gulfs between the spheres that should not have existed in the first place. In fact, without the other spheres, each is impotent with respect to innovation. We must break the centrifugal force of habit that impels and binds each sphere in role-prescriptive paths of interaction. As the district becomes a center of inquiry, everyone "on-site" in the district becomes responsible for student and collegial learning. Teamwork becomes reality: from team teaching, to interdisciplinary units, to seminars and workshops led by students, teachers, administrators, and community members.

Of all the areas where the literature is converging, perhaps the most arresting is the remarkable degree of agreement about the need for integrating the spheres of the organization, from the early studies of the organizational context of innovation (Berman and McLaughlin 1975) to Loucks-Horsley's (1987) recent statements. Huberman (1992), Louis and Miles (1990), and Fullan and Miles (1991) have come to the conclusion that the levels of the system have to work together (not simply be coordinated) to ensure effective staff development and, thus, school improvement.

Many researchers have documented the incredible isolation of teachers from teachers (Lortie, Rosenholtz, Little), teachers from principals (Leithwood, Bossert, Rowan, Fullan, Hargreaves), principals from principals (Leithwood, Baldridge, Deal), and schools from central offices (Fullan, Deal), and the resulting fragmented socioprofessional system of education. More successful schools (Mortimore, Brookover, Levine and Lezotte) and schools embodying more successful initiatives for school improvement (Rosenholtz, Huberman and Miles, Hopkins, Louis and Miles) possess greater degrees of cohesion and more collaborative structures. In addition, teachers, building administrators, and central offices are closer together and have relations conducive to mutual support. Hence the emphasis on "co-leadership."

Some types of proposals for "site-based" management have accentuated the divisions between spheres, advocating virtual autonomy for schools, with the assumption that central office personnel only inhibit the creativity and synergy of the schools. Recent studies of innovation and change have come to a far different conclusion—that, without support from the district office personnel, few schools successfully engage in school improvement (Huberman and Miles 1984, 1986; Louis and Miles 1990; Fullan and Miles 1991). Even where school faculties identify curricular and instructional initiatives, schoolwide implementation is virtually impossible without facilitation and support from the district.

The three spheres are mutually interdependent. The self-renewing school or district lives as a cooperative venture—all members of the organization share the raw responsibility of educating thousands of young people. Without broad cooperation, faculties and central offices are equally impotent when it comes to making significant changes. Faculties not supported by administrators, trainers, and organizers have great difficulty, with rare exceptions, overcoming the alienation produced by the extreme autonomy of the workplace. District offices not closely connected to teachers and schools are unable to create the conditions to support change.

The Importance of Leadership

In self-renewing schools, vigorous, integrative leadership, supportive and exhortative in appropriate measures, is generated at all levels. A corollary is the development of within-organization capability for training (as represented by a cadre that crosses role groups).

For a few years, segments of the school-improvement literature accentuated differences between district initiatives and those made by teachers. Many researchers made distinctions between "top down" and "bottom up" initiatives and suggested that initiatives by teachers would be more effective because "buy-in" would be ensured. Studies of schools and teachers engaged in action research (David and Peterson 1984, Calhoun 1992, Calhoun and Glickman 1993) and studies of teachers who volunteered for training (Hopkins 1990), however, have made it clear that many schools have difficulty making initiatives in curriculum and instruction even when funded substantially (as in the case of the California School Improvement Program)—unless they have strong leadership.

Strong leadership at the school level seems to be essential, whether teachers are generating initiatives or implementing ones created at other levels of the organization. All schools need leadership teams connected to district councils of teachers. Schools also need administrators with broad responsibility for overseeing the health of the organization, making and coordinating initiatives, and governing the cadre (the technical unit that provides support within the organization).

Two important dimensions of leadership have been accentuated in the recent research on the dynamics of school faculties:

• First, the ability to generate a collaborative community is extremely important (Levine and Lezotte 1990; Glickman 1990; Barth 1991a, b). The most effective leadership is not embodied in a "strong man or woman" who manipulates others, but in the ability to generate a democratic framework and process that binds the organization productively.

• Second, the most effective leaders do not simply follow established formulas for getting things done, but are effective diagnosticians, problem solvers, and leaders of others to find needs and create solutions. do not simply follow established formulas for getting things done, but are effective diagnosticians, problem solvers, and leaders of others to find needs and create solutions.

In both dimensions, leaders understand the development of their community and its members and work to generate the capability of those they are designated to lead (Leithwood 1990).

The Integration of Initiatives

In the self-renewing school, priorities and coordination guide decision making to ensure that initiatives in curriculum, instruction, and technology support one another and that excessive numbers of initiatives are not engaged in at any one time.

Attempts to create better learning environments for children constitute much of the activity of the organization. From sweeping curriculum changes to each interchange in the classroom, every act needs to be imbued with the spirit that seeks excellence. To accomplish such intensity requires careful prioritization and integration.

Self-renewing schools discard the practice of lightly supported, fragmented initiatives. When all three spheres—teacher, school, and district—are legitimized and encouraged to generate initiatives, staff members soon find that setting priorities and coordinating are essential to the self-renewing organization. A good rule of thumb is that the organization as a whole will be able to manage one major initiative each year or two, the faculty about one each year, and the teacher about one additional initiative a year. Operationally, the product will be impressive. Imagine that the whole organization integrated the computer into educational practice during a two-year period while each school was making a significant improvement in a curriculum area and every teacher was adding two important teaching strategies to his repertoire! Scheduling initiatives in such a way allows for proper support. What a difference from our current mode, with dozens of lightly supported initiatives landing on everyone pell mell.

The energy from the three spheres of the organization can, if not coordinated, easily overfill the relatively little time currently available for the cooperative planning and staff development necessary to support initiatives. People can feel frustration as ideas interfere with one another or are given less attention than they need. Staff members in all three spheres should develop planning mechanisms to prioritize and coordinate initiatives. These mechanisms should be designed to minimize unintended conflict and to promote action and continuous assessment. They should be designed to support one another. In the past, initiatives in curriculum and instruction often competed for time and energy. When a curricular initiative is made in one area, say, for example, writing, any initiative in instruction needs to be shaped to support the implementation in the curriculum area.

Three findings from the research are especially relevant to this principle:

1. Districts tend to generate many initiatives simultaneously but superficially (Loucks-Horsley et al. 1987, Fullan and Steigelbauer 1991).

2. A multitude of lightly supported initiatives gives teachers and principals a feeling of being inundated by an impossible array of demands "from above," and everyone is frustrated by the lack of implementation (Cuban 1990, Goodlad 1984, Rosenholtz 1989, Fullan and Steigelbauer 1991, Little 1990) Teachers end up feeling alienated and pushed around.

3. The lack of integration among the spheres or levels of the system leaves schools and teachers unsure about what they are supposed to emphasize and how much initiative they are to take. The result is confusion and cynicism (Sarason 1990).

Carefully staged initiatives are in order, with clear understanding about their relationship to schools and teachers (and the role of teachers and schools in making initiatives of their own). Doing fewer things well benefits the organization and the students. A corollary is that efforts in curriculum, instruction, technology, and school climate should be integrated or, at least, should support one another. The long history of officially "adopting" sweeping changes in one curriculum area after another and failing to achieve implementation needs to be ended forthwith.

The Design of Initiatives in Curriculum, Instruction, and Technology

In self-renewing schools, the entire organization conducts action research, enabling teachers, schools, and the organization to study themselves as they make initiatives for the improvement of student learning.

Research-based training designs should be used to learn new things. Designs need to include follow-up in the workplace, ensuring implementation and studying effects on students. Training should make explicit how various initiatives support one another. Self-renewing organizations simply need to create the conditions that enable people to learn effectively. The means are at hand, but have been underused. Effective training requires that workshops and courses contain the appropriate proportions of demonstrations, study of rationale, and practice. The workplace must be organized to ensure that participants are allowed to practice until they achieve competence with any new procedure (Joyce and Showers 1988). Also, implementation needs to be studied very carefully and follow-up training adjusted according to the results, as part of the action research process.

The summaries of research on training (Lawrence 1974, Sparks 1983) provide some really good news—that properly designed workshops and follow-up enable virtually all teachers to learn and implement even the most complex changes in instruction and curriculum. Included in the procedures are substantial changes in relationships among teachers. Hence, the effective training procedures cannot be effectively implemented unless the social organization of faculties and patterns of leadership change radically. Fortunately, the implementation of effective training procedures has positive effects on the workplace, increasing collegiality and positive relationships between teachers and administrators.

The use of effective designs for training involves a considerable shift from the frequent practice of trying to make major changes with minor attention to what it takes for people to learn and integrate new content and teaching procedures into their active repertoires. The best antidote is for all personnel to understand the technical aspects of change, especially how to acquire the teaching skills and strategies needed when any major change is made. In a real sense, everyone needs to be a designer of training, understanding the place that demonstration and practice have in the acquisition of new skills. As things currently stand, curriculum planners frequently provide one or two days of explanation to support a sweeping curriculum change (such as "whole" or "integrated" language programs) without appearing to realize that the result is frustration—with very little implementation. Similarly, many teachers do not realize how to work through the periods of awkwardness and anxiety that accompany learning new instructional procedures. A curriculum change in a major area probably requires ten to fifteen days of training, rather than the one or two that are often provided now. We have to exit our "pretend world" where groups of teachers and administrators adopt complex curriculum changes, provide brief training, accept low implementation levels, and label the result as "curriculum change." One reason some scholars of American education (such as Sarason and Cuban) are so pessimistic about its ability to make changes that affect students is that the relatively obvious need for adequate training has been neglected for so long and in so many places.

One reason that many schools and districts have not instituted better design is that many people blame the motivation (or lack thereof) of teachers for failures of implementation. We often substitute both poor motivation and lack of "buy-in" as explanations for why procedures and content are or are not implemented. The organization has often used lack of teacher motivation to explain low levels of implementation, whereas adequate training would have achieved higher levels. *The very important finding from the Huberman and Miles (1984) studies that commitment follows competence needs to be taken seriously.* Until you are good at something, you have little idea how you will like it. On the other hand, something that appears attractive on first acquaintance may not wear well. However, competence generally builds commitment. Also, with good training design, virtually all teachers reach adequate levels of competence. Researchers have found that poor design of training and implementation, rather than poor motivation, was the reason for low levels of implementation.

The origins of an innovation have little to do with the need for training. If teachers have an idea for a change, just as much training is needed as if the idea had originated elsewhere in one of the other spheres. The same is true if all participants are volunteers. Sometimes it is thought that if an innovation starts with volunteers, they will have an easier time learning how to implement it. However, although working with volunteers is very pleasant, voluntary participants have to engage in the same amounts of study and practice as does anyone else. There are some spectacular reports of nonimplementation where the participants were all volunteers who had "bought in," but either the design of training was poor or the use of study groups and peer coaching was omitted (Hopkins 1990). As Sarason (1990) and Cuban (1990) point out, somewhat acerbically, the beautifully designed curriculums of the Academic Reform Movement and the promises of educational technology have both dissipated because they were disseminated under the principle that a few enthusiastic volunteers could somehow carry the day without support. As Cuban and Sarason emphasize, these mistakes do not have to be repeated. Let us briefly examine the training elements that can be combined to provide a high probability of decent implementation.

We make a distinction between the design of workshops, which need to develop a degree of knowledge and skill that will sustain practice in the school, and the design of the workplace—the conditions in school that enable practitioners to work together until they have mastered the teaching skills that are the content of the training. The two designs need to be integrated, but the problems of organizing them are considerably different. The following section examines the principal components of the design of training (the workshop time): the lectures, readings, and discussions created to develop theoretical understanding; the demonstrations designed to provide behavioral descriptions of the procedures; and provisions for initial practice in the workshop. A later section discusses conditions necessary for implementation in the workplace.

Design of the Workshop

Development of Theoretical Understanding

Understanding sustains best use, unless practice is to be rote and formulaic. Teachers need to know the conceptual base and have a thorough understanding of the kinds of effects they can expect if they appropriately follow certain variations of a teaching model or strategy. They also need to know how to measure progress to determine if they are getting the desired effects. In other words, in the well-designed workshop, "trainers" and other participants become an action research team. *We find that the general theory and the knowledge of expected effects are underemphasized in many workshops.* Yet, without deep understanding, an innovation will be short-lived (see Fullan and Steigelbauer 1991, Joyce and Showers 1988, and Showers 1989 for extensive treatments). Knowledge of the expected magnitude of effects on student learning is extremely important, for it keeps the purpose of the training in the forefront.

Development of theoretical understanding also supports variations of the teaching strategy and curriculum not included in initial training. For example, people learning their first cooperative learning technique should not deceive themselves that they have understood everything about the strategy. They are just beginning their venture.

Behavioral Representations: Modeling and Demonstration

The fulcrum of training design is demonstration. The research evidence is substantial (see Borg, Kallenback, Morris, and Friebel 1969; Joyce, Peck, and Brown 1982; McDonald 1973). Modeling anchors the theory in clarified behavior and provides the behavioral basis for skill development. Demonstrating with the teachers as "students" is useful but is no substitute for videotapes of children working in cooperative groups. Especially needed are tapes showing how to organize the students and provide them with instructions.

How much demonstration is needed? We currently estimate that about twenty demonstrations are needed as a base for adequate skill development for a medium-complexity model of teaching. At least half of these demonstrations should be videotapes with students. In our current work, we employ about a dozen tapes to demonstrate even the simplest of techniques. Trainers need to keep in mind that when participants engage in their first trials in the classroom, they tend to mimic closely what they have seen in training. Thus, although demonstrations at an adult level are very useful, they should not be relied on exclusively.

Practice

Trainers need to provide opportunities for practice within the workshop setting. Teachers new to a procedure need practice, especially in making the "opening moves" that start a teaching-learning episode. Skillful demonstrators bring the students into the process so smoothly that people who are novices have trouble profiting from that aspect of the demonstration. Practice of the process during the workshop gives the trainer the opportunity to observe and to follow up these observations with further demonstrations that make critical skills manifest.

The combination of these three elements—providing for theoretical understanding, demonstration, and initial practice—enables nearly all teachers to develop a level of skill that will sustain practice in the classroom (Showers 1989); but the process of transfer to the workplace has just begun. *If nothing else is done, fewer than 10 percent of the teachers will be able to engage in enough practice to add the new procedures to their repertoire* (Joyce and Showers 1988). Thus, the design of the workplace and opportunities to practice after the workshop are crucial to the success of teachers in implementing a new strategy.

The Design of the Workplace

Teachers need a mixture of understandings and procedures if they are to be successful in transferring skills practiced in the workshop to their classroom instruction. Up-front design of the workplace—as part of the initial planning and funding, prior to the workshop—helps ensure that workshop participants will have the assistance they need to navigate the distance between the training setting and the instructional setting. In the course of this process of transfer, their understandings will deepen; their skills will mature; and, central to transfer, their understanding of when to use the procedure and how to increase the skills of the learner will develop. It may be useful to think about designing the workplace for successful implementation as similar to establishing the conditions to support learning in a great classroom.

What have we learned thus far about the transfer of teaching strategies or curricular patterns practiced in the workshop setting to the skillful use or appropriate implementation of these strategies in the classroom? Thus far in our own inquiry into practice, we know that the design of the workplace must include provisions for immediate and sustained classroom practice, companionship and peer coaching, and the study of implementation.

Immediate and Sustained Practice

The first understanding is that practice needs to be immediate and sustained. Delaying practice inevitably leads to a loss of understanding and skill among workshop participants. If there is any fear or skepticism about the use of the new procedure, delay gives anxiety time to develop; and practice will not ensue. Thus, immediate practice is essential.

Second, people need twenty to thirty trials with any new procedure before they achieve control and comfort with the procedure. Teachers also need to understand that the anxiety that often accompanies initial practice will diminish rapidly after the first half-dozen trials. Otherwise, they will tend to avoid the anxiety by avoiding practice. Also, most people feel less competent as they practice new skills, for both cognition and skills are being acquired. Foreknowledge and discussion of this uncertainty or discomfort can provide individual and collective support and help sustain practice. During the "awkward" stage, when people expend so much energy concentrating on the activities, teachers tend to see this stage as an end in itself—"getting through" the activity feels like quite enough of a goal at the moment. As people attain comfort in the new skill, the *actual* goal—to provide tools to the learner—needs to rise again to a central place. Just doing new activities (using new teaching strategies mechanically) will not achieve the purpose of increasing student opportunity to learn (Joyce, Showers, and Weil 1992, Chapter 1).

Sharing and Peer Coaching

Companionship and sharing (as in peer coaching) will greatly boost implementation. Thus, *before training*, teachers need to organize themselves into study groups who will share plans, discuss their experiences, and develop a sense of community as they struggle to bring about change. Observation is very helpful, for it enables members of study groups to pick up ideas from one another and to get a sense of their relative success; however, study group members should be chary of offering advice to one another. They need to acknowledge that they are novices with the new procedure and may well offer poor advice without realizing it. We have watched more than one study group invent a dysfunctional variation on cooperative learning because the most forthcoming member of the group provided the wrong advice in a knowing manner.

Immediate and sustained practice, combined with companionship and focused discussion and boosted by observation, will ensure that nearly all participants will reach a routine but mechanical level of use with the new procedure. Provided that practice occurs daily, this level should bet reached in about six weeks and create readiness for the next workshop, which should occur about then (Showers 1989).

Before training begins, both participants and organizers should make a commitment to immediate practice at the workplace. District or school organizers need to provide time for study groups to meet, facilitate observations, and communicate any problems to the trainer.

Studying Implementation

All personnel need to keep track of numbers of classroom practices, the content of study-group meetings, and degrees of implementation by participants. Self-report "logs" of use and "minutes" of study-group meetings are important data sources for formative assessment (action research). Participants can also collect instructional materials. We have found it useful to help teachers track their own perceptions of their growing level of confidence with any procedure, as well as their students' competence with it. Teachers, "trainers," and organizers all need to know where implementation stands at any given time, when more help is needed, and what is going well—and poorly.

The study of implementation enables celebrations of progress. Simple acknowledgment that "our whole staff is now using cooperative procedures regularly" counts for a lot in building a sense of collective efficacy. Sharing data about problems encountered enables people to understand that they are not the only ones who struggle. These data also enable everyone to get a realistic picture of their effectiveness and to plan workshops tailored to progress and problems. Otherwise proper support is hard to design.

The study of implementation not only facilitates the design of support but also helps trainers and organizers determine when participants have reached a level of competence in a given procedure and thus need no more training in that particular strategy. This happens when participants reach "executive control" and use the procedure strongly, sensitively, and for appropriate objectives. In studies with several models of teaching, we have found that the effects on student learning are dramatically higher when teachers reach executive control than they are when teachers only use the procedures routinely (see, e.g., Joyce, Murphy, Showers, and Murphy 1989).

The design of the workplace, establishing conditions known to support successful implementation, sets us up to make the changes we desire for the education of our students. The lack of such a design establishes, instead, the conditions for failure and frustration. These conditions should be designed and funded prior to the initial workshops. If the district or school personnel cannot "afford" the time and financial commitment for follow-up support, they should delay initiation. We must give up the operational belief that good intentions and wishful implementation will support desirable changes in education. No other profession expects so much knowledge and skill from its initiates or so much from its veterans with such meager in-depth preparation. Of the twenty or more most powerful teaching strategies that cross subject areas and have a historical track record of high payoff in terms of student effects, we speculate that fewer than 10 percent of us—kindergarten through university level—regularly employ more than one of these strategies (see Bellack 1963, Goodlad 1984, Sadker and Sadker 1985). We believe that schools can change this speculative statistic rapidly, to the great benefit of their students.

Motivation

As we mentioned earlier in this chapter, participants in any new initiative in education must remember that commitment follows competence (Huberman and Miles 1984). Trying to seduce participants into commitment before they are good at something is to set them up for disappointment, simply because the early trials are likely to feel awkward and are likely to be accompanied by anxiety. Regular practice, however, will fix those natural problems. After becoming reasonably competent, the participant can decide how committed to get. Similarly, success by a small group within a school does not effectively spread an innovative practice, as we know from years of supervisory experience; but good training and a few weeks of regular practice can lead to schoolwide use of worthy innovations. Everyone who teaches possesses sufficient motivation to respond to good design of training and supportive conditions in the workplace.

5 Re-Creating the System

HOW DO WE GO ABOUT BUILDING A SELF-RENEWING ORGANIZA-
tion? how do we turn our system into an academy? While acknowledging that this process will not be easy, we can make substantial
changes relatively quickly. A central premise is that all the spheres—
individual teachers, schools, and districts—engage in a series of
action research inquiries, generating and studying the effects of
initiatives for school improvement. When we pursue these inquiries,
changes occur in the collegial relationships within and across
spheres; and support systems are developed that can sustain renewal
throughout the system.

Strategy for Building Self-Renewing Schools

To begin this way of working and learning together, we suggest
a rather simple, straightforward strategy. Even as we use it, the
strategy is a subject for research—for we are not finished learning
how to build self-renewing educational organizations.

Four strands characterize this strategy. The first two are proce-
dural and have to do with *how* things are done. One of these is altering
how we conduct initiatives for school improvement—essentially so
that each initiative generates changes in the system and its operations.
The second is making action research a basic mode of operation for
everyone in the organization.

The third and fourth strands are structural and have to do with the
organizational framework: the establishment of a generic cadre for
school renewal and the organization of leadership teams and study
groups within the schools.

Strand 1. Altering How School Improvement Initiatives Are Conducted

We can build in an evolutionary manner on the best features of our current practices. Regularly, each sphere will generate initiatives to improve various aspects of curriculum, instruction, and technology. Each initiative is conducted so that its implementation enhances the self-renewing capability of our academy. For example, when we initiate a change in the curriculum, we put into practice some of the principles and practices that represent the new system. We coordinate the initiative with other major activities, and we take care to ensure that it does not contribute to "initiative overload." The training is adequate in quantity; and the cadre designs staff development according to the results of the research on training. The faculties are organized into study groups to implement the new curriculum. Leadership teams within the school are prepared to explain the curriculum and changes in the workplace, a function they will perform for other initiatives in the future. The initiative is a focus for action research.

By conducting each initiative in this fashion, we can build the organization's capability for self-renewal by increments. In addition, with each successful initiative, the sense of collective efficacy should build for each study group, faculty, and the system as a whole. People should discover that they can actually make changes and make them well. By designing each initiative according to principles that make it highly probable that success will occur, we are trying to do what good classroom teachers do to set their students up for success—by tending to individual needs and balancing multiple goals simultaneously.

Strand 2. Doing Things the Action-Research Way

The schools and the district engage in action research on a study team basis, on a schoolwide basis, and on a districtwide basis. Using schoolwide action research as an example, faculty members select an area or problem of collective interest; collect, organize, and interpret on-site data related to this area; and take action based on their interpretation of the data (Calhoun 1991, Glickman 1990). The process serves as formative evaluation of the effects of schoolwide actions. To support major initiatives and to benefit from the collective wisdom of other educators and institutions, schoolwide action research includes a study of the available professional literature, to combine its information with the results of on-site data.

Study groups play a major role in transforming our professional literature into information for use at the classroom and school level. The combination of information the faculty is collecting and analyzing about their school, juxtaposed with the information they are collecting and analyzing from the professional literature, leads to more informed decisions. Such disciplined inquiry, involving all members of the organization, enhances professional growth and provides the group with the knowledge needed to select actions for achieving commonly valued goals.

Strand 3. Developing a Generic Cadre

A school involved in improvement efforts should immediately form—and prepare—a core group (cadre) to facilitate change. This cadre, composed of teachers, building administrators, and district office personnel, needs to develop the capability to provide service to the principals, school-based leadership teams, central office staff, and teachers in many areas, rather than being an ad hoc creation to serve one initiative. The functions of the cadre include:

1. Providing training on generic teaching skills and many models of teaching.

2. Providing training on the implementation of curriculum.

3. Building the capacity of leadership teams to organize the faculties into productive problem-solving teams, including the organization of study groups to ensure the implementation of changes in curriculum and instruction.

4. Developing training materials and procedures, including creating training for innovations that emerge as priorities.

5. Applying understanding of the change process to curricular and instructional innovation and helping all personnel understand change.

6. Studying implementation and supporting individuals progressing through the stages of concern as they work their way from awkwardness to executive control of new content and teaching strategies.

7. Facilitating action research throughout the organization.

This generic cadre serves in a leadership role and as an operational model: As a unit, it embodies the collegial learning and experimentation we wish to create at all levels of the organization. The creation of continuous growth and school renewal requires changes in how we live, think, and interact with each other. The cadre is the facilitator of the transformation: learning, instructing, nurturing, and supporting individual, school, and district initiatives.

Strand 4. Organizing Leadership Teams and Study Groups

Two school-based groups facilitate individual and organizational change—leadership teams and study groups. The leadership team, composed of teachers and administrators, works with the faculty to identify areas for school improvement, collect data, make school-relevant initiatives, and study the effects of those initiatives. Although only a few faculty members belong to the leadership team during any one period of time, all members always belong to a study group. Study groups of four to six members work together on the same basis—selecting areas for study, making initiatives, and assessing them. Group members study the professional literature and reflect on it, engage in staff development together, use peer coaching to support their transfer of skills and content to the workplace, and conduct joint study of what is happening in their classrooms and to initiatives made by the faculty working as a whole. Thus the schools engage in action research on a schoolwide basis, with study teams as the center.

Integrating the School and the District

During the beginning stages of a self-renewing school's improvement efforts, people in all spheres pay a great deal of attention to creating integrative relationships both among people and among previously separated spheres.

District offices need to provide nurturing environments for the school renewal process. Their personnel should make it obvious, from what they pay attention to and from what they fund, that the pursuit of instructional effectiveness is valued (Blum and Kneidek 1991). In fact, we think that every district office professional should participate as an active member in one school's change process. Clear policies, expectations for improvement, and a strong system of support all help schools and districts become stronger organizations. Acknowledging joint responsibility for school renewal—at individual, school, and district levels—is a major first step in changing the culture of our workplace.

Levine (1991), summarizing findings and implications from research on effective schools, succinctly describes this joint collaboration: "The success of an effective school program depends on a judicious mixture of autonomy for participating faculties and control from the central office, a kind of 'directed autonomy' " (p. 392). In a reciprocal way, the schools do not behave as if they were separate school systems, but call on the cadre for support for their school-based initiatives and cooperate with district initiatives.

In the self-renewing organization as we can conceive it at present, central office personnel coordinate initiatives, help the generic cadre interface with the schools, generate initiatives specific to the character and needs of the district, and maintain the focus on student learning and collective inquiry. They ensure adequate preparation for the cadre, and they support the cadre and receive support from the group as it leads action research for the district.

Another important function of central offices is to ensure equity of learning opportunities throughout the district (Corbett and Wilson 1991). One of the delicate dimensions of relationships between schools and district personnel is that the district sphere needs to encourage and support initiatives from all the schools. At the same time, the district must provide support to ensure that no school offers significantly poorer quality of education than do the others (some schools may be working harder at renewal than others).

Site-Based School Improvement and the Self-Renewing Organization

How does our proposal for re-creating the system fit into the current wave of site-based school improvement? That movement has drawn attention to the need to transform the way we work together. With the movement toward school-based management, the roles and relationships of district/central office personnel and school personnel have come under greater scrutiny. This self-examination and public review of school management can be used to create healthier schools and districts. As we seek to renew our system for public education, our titles, roles, and functions may blur and change as people in each sphere of the organization become more united and more oriented to accomplishments than to job descriptions. Such change may create confusion and, sometimes, even fear of loss of control or loss of power. Because we are all engaged in the study of change, however, we can remind ourselves and our colleagues that such reactions are natural as new patterns of interaction evolve.

Continuity with Change

Maintaining the organization while learning new ways of working together is another delicate process. The organization has to keep going while changing, and some of the things that are accomplished regularly have to continue. Drucker (1985) points out that the act of continuing can subvert the act of change, but also that chaos in the organization can abort change efforts equally quickly. For example, schools need to continue to graduate students even while in the process of changing graduation requirements. In the planning scenario we present in Part II, many of the activities "sound like" common practice—and in many ways they are, because they fill needs that keep the organization afloat. *The trick is to manage familiar functions in such a way that they are subtly altered in line with the desired directions for change.*

Selecting Initiatives

Of all the decisions people make in a self-renewing organization, probably none is more important than selecting initiatives that will pay off in terms of student learning. Teachers as individuals, schools as faculties, and district personnel as coordinators need to be parsimonious about the number of initiatives that are on the table at any one time. Personnel in all three spheres need to use the limited time and energy available on projects that will have a positive impact. To increase the capacity for innovation and then select weak initiatives would be tragic.

Selecting options to explore takes us beyond technical knowledge of the alternatives and the research underlying them. The task of sorting out initiatives from various sources is formidable, especially because so many people and groups are concerned about the quality of education and are making proposals to improve it. Our selection process requires us to include a vision of the purposes of education in the larger society, one that makes the function of the schools and their moral purpose a central role in the choices we make.

A Bombardment of Proposals

A few years ago, a story circulated that the major problem with the Sunday *New York Times* was that it took all day Sunday to read it. Today we have a similar problem getting through the masses of newsprint and catalogs advertising ways of fixing education. Suggestions and recommendations pour from the press, formal citizens' groups, state and national legislative and executive branches, professional organizations, and a large coterie of consultant firms. You barely finish reading the pile of clippings and fliers from one month before the mailperson staggers in with the next heap.

Not since the '60s have American schools been bombarded with so much advice—or such a *variety* of counsel—about what will make them better. Nor have the voices calling for school improvement been so insistent. Just the assortment of sources is dizzying.

Citizens' organizations and the public press advise the schools, focusing on the questions of their greatest concern, such as literacy, international economic competitiveness, and basic skills. Both citizens' groups and reporters can advocate several reforms simultaneously, including somewhat contradictory ones. For example, the same article can contain arguments for an end of "tracking" and a separate call for the expansion of advanced-placement courses for selected students—without reconciling the potential inconsistencies between the two.

Legislation and gubernatorial pronouncements advocate both specific and general approaches to school improvement. These approaches range from "mandates" to improve "test scores" to the provision of resources to provide special services to students with special needs, such as students for whom English is a second language. Changes in funding structures, including varieties of "voucher" plans, are very popular. Many concerned people believe that competitive structures will cause the schools to generate improvement without specifying the nature of the changes. Some prominent political figures lobby for market economy approaches and imply that the privatization of education will generate school improvement efforts.

Through journals, tapes, workshops, and advertisements, professional organizations and vendors of training strew the schools with proposals about what to change and how to do it. Some of the ideas, such as nongrading, team teaching, and interdisciplinary curriculums, have been around for a while and are resurfacing. Others are recent developments. They are not easy to sort out, both because of the quantity and because the same terms can refer to some really quite different proposals. *Restructuring* is a good example. As Elmore (1990) has pointed out, this term can refer to political, collegial, or curricular and instructional proposals. The word *restructuring* leads all others in both current usage and in the difficulty of sorting out its many meanings.

Sorting out the alternatives is a task in itself. From all sources, we are inundated with proposals concerning:

1. General strategies for school renewal
2. The organization of support systems for implementing change, including the design of staff development and the selection of content for it
4. Curricular variations
5. Instructional models and skills
6. Ways of grouping teachers and students for instruction
7. Types and uses of assessment
8. The governance of budgets and schools

Let's look at proposals from the professional sector—educational organizations and consultants. Many school-improvement proposals from these groups involve global change: how to reorganize and operate schools. We see basketfuls of "site-based" approaches to staff development and school renewal, as well as the promotion of "reflective practice," "strategic planning," "management by objectives," and "total quality management." Some of these approaches are thought to be compatible by their advocates, whereas the advocates of others are in opposition to one another. A number of quite different strategies are called "action research" (Calhoun 1992, Oja and Smulyan 1989).

Other proposals pertain to curricular content and instruction and technological devices. Professional organizations are currently emphasizing technologies, especially "multimedia." Another current emphasis is the use of alternative strategies for assessment, particularly attempts to create curriculum-relevant, realistic, or "authentic" ones—as opposed to standardized testing or paper-and-pencil tests. Varieties of cooperative learning have been going strong for a decade, along with a number of approaches to teaching "thinking skills" and suggestions for approaching curriculum content in ways that enhance the powers of thought of both students and teachers. Many organizations are focusing on alternative approaches to language arts through several important but somewhat loosely defined systems, such as "literature-based language arts," "whole language," and "integrated language arts." Multicultural education is prominent again, and global education is struggling to become so. Curriculum-area organizations are on the move. The National Council of Teachers of Mathematics has stimulated activity in that curriculum area with the recent publicity given their newest "standards." We can expect a variety of interpretations of these mathematics standards, as well as the new framework from the National Council for the Social Studies.

Teaching gets a reasonable amount of attention from some organizations, including the International Reading Association and the Association for Supervision and Curriculum Development. Such organizations promote varieties of models of teaching (see Joyce, Showers, and Weil 1992); and various teaching skills [e.g., Teacher Expectations and Student Achievement (TESA)] and "essential" elements of instruction maintain fairly good market shares, as do a variety of approaches to mastery learning.

Picking Through the Maze

In this discussion of the possibilities for school change, we attempt to illustrate what might happen were policymakers to engage in a thorough search of the literature undergirding the proposals that various organizations are currently making. Whether policymakers represent states, counties, intermediate agencies, districts, or schools, a major task is to learn about the available courses of action, weigh their possible benefits, and select ones to be used. The problem-solving process is the same for people in all sorts of roles—governors, superintendents, organizers of staff development, principals, and teachers as faculties and as teacher organizations—in discovering which school-improvement approaches work and how well they work. And there is a large literature that can help them.

Decision makers need to grasp the possibilities and, before choosing one approach—or any combination—for the school or district to pursue, try to find out what difference the proposed change might make to student growth. Assessing the history of the proposals and their likelihood of paying off requires energy. Simply accepting the promises of advocates is unsatisfactory. All the alternatives have champions, whether or not the idea has been tested—but decisions have to be made about the ones that will focus energy for serious school improvement programs.

The central criterion for selection needs to be what holds the greatest promise for children. Student learning is the objective of education. A significant proportion of the proposals skirt that objective and will generate apparent rather than real change, leaving business to be conducted as usual behind a facade of reform. We have to pick our way around these by keeping the focus on student learning central. Otherwise, the entire decision-making process is subverted.

Our accessible knowledge base is uneven—appallingly so, in that some long-advocated avenues have been little studied. Yet, if you dig around long enough, there is a good deal of evidence available about many proposed avenues; and some of the results are eye-openers about what works and what doesn't. A useful tool to use in processing the mass of published research is the procedure for determining "effect size" introduced by Glass (1982). The concept of effect size enables us to compare the results of studies done under differing conditions with dissimilar treatments and thus weigh the effects of alternatives more accurately than previously. As Part II of this book shows, the procedure can be invaluable for policymakers who are willing to become serious students of educational research.

PART II

MAKING IT HAPPEN

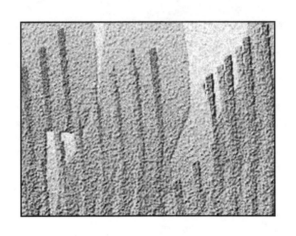

6

The District Restructuring Committee: Scene One— Preparing for Action

ASSUMING THAT THE PRINCIPLES OF THE SELF-RENEWING ORGANIZATION are reasonably sound and that—mixed with ingenuity, organizational acumen, and a lot of hard work—they provide a core of ideas on which we can begin to build our self-renewing organization, what else do we need to consider? We suggest asking two questions:

• How do we guide the process so that the campaign to create a better education for the students is blended effectively with the drive to create a better workplace for educators?

• How do we permeate the process with the disciplined inquiry that will locate the best educational practices that have emerged through research and innovation?

In Part II of this book, we review some of the researched storehouse of possibilities. The chapters that follow are not a guideline for selection from all the possibilities; rather, we wish to facilitate thinking about options and alternatives. We have structured Part II as a scenario in which the leaders of a district begin the movement to change their organizational culture. In the context of the scenario, we explore many of the curricular, instructional, and organizational options that are currently available; identify the research underlying these approaches; and analyze why some options appear to pay off and others don't.

Forming the Restructuring Committee

In our imagination, we now shift to the setting of a school district and attend a series of meetings intended to generate serious efforts to restructure the educational process and the shape of the workplace. Participants have made a commitment to draw on the literature on change, curriculum, instruction, and technology. Our initial meetings are attended by the superintendent and associate superintendents for curriculum and staff development, their support staff (the "cabinet" of a typical school district), and teams of principals and teachers. (Obviously, the numbers of people involved and the complexity of the process will vary by the size of the district.) Our restructuring committee begins by studying the general literature on school renewal and innovation. Let's see what they find.

Studies of Successful School Renewal

From their reading and study, committee members make five significant discoveries.

1. There Is Good Research Available.

Many curricular, instructional, and technological models have been well researched and have demonstrated effects on student learning. Our restructuring committee also discovers that, where significant improvement has happened, it has happened rapidly.

The big message is that there is cause for optimism because our committee finds options that will pay off, and the participants realize that innovations can be implemented and gains seen in student achievement within a year. That many attempts to improve schooling have stumbled and eventually been dissipated is of little consequence, because our committee can pay attention to the approaches that work and work fast.

2. Curriculum, Instruction, and Technology Are Central in the Programs That Have Brought About Positive Change.

All the reported programs that succeeded in having positive effects on student learning included changes in instruction, curriculum, or technologies. Changes in structures of governance or planning have not affected student learning unless they resulted in modifications in content or instructional process. For example, moving from centralized to site-based decision making, while it may be desirable for a variety of other reasons, will not increase student learning unless the faculties decide to make changes in what is taught and how it is learned. Faculties that are unaccustomed to taking collective action in curriculum and instruction—and that is most of them—will have difficulty as they learn to do so, and the majority will need help with process and substance. Although there are good professional reasons for increasing collegial decision making, it is neither an easy nor a short route to increased student learning (see, e.g., Brophy 1992; David and Peterson 1984; Huberman and Miles 1986; Louis and Miles 1990).

3. Effective Staff Development and General Support Systems Are Essential.

All the reported instances where student learning has increased have included substantial amounts of technical assistance to help faculties develop a rigorous and supportive process for decision making. Then, after they make decisions, faculties need staff development and technical assistance to support implementation. Our restructuring committee also discover that not just any kind of staff development will suffice. *Many common forms of staff development result in implementation in as few as 10 percent of the classrooms, whereas certain tested designs for workshops and follow-up in the workplace improve use to 90 percent or more.* The design of effective support following initial training sessions requires careful study, for such support is essential for major curricular and instructional implementation (see, e.g., Bennett 1987, Fullan 1990, Joyce and Showers 1988, Levine 1991, Pink 1989, Showers 1989.)

4. Successful School Improvement Requires the Participation of All, or Nearly All, of the People Involved.

In whatever segment of the organization that is trying to improve, all personnel need to participate in the initiative. A few enthusiastic volunteers do not a school-improvement program make. Schoolwide participation is essential where the school is the focus; and districtwide participation, where the education agency is the focus (see, e.g., Pajak and Glickman 1989, Fullan 1991, Fullan and Steigelbauer 1991, Miles 1992).

5. Embedded Formative Evaluation Is Essential to Successful Initiatives.

Not surprisingly, our committee finds that successful school improvement efforts included the study of the use of the innovations—how much actually changed—and the effects on student learning. A system for tracking effects was put in place early and used to confirm or modify the innovation while it was in progress. The effects on students were examined at regular intervals spaced fairly closely together. As the committee examines the successful programs, they find that some assessments were as frequent as weekly (referrals and disciplinary action are examples of very frequent readings of progress); others were as far apart as quarterly (quality of writing is an example).

Our restructuring committee finds that successful school improvement programs do not wait for the standard "test scores" to come in. Those are used for confirmation of what has already been documented. Implementation of curriculum, instruction, and technologies has often been so uneven that the assessment of effects has been virtually meaningless. Only very careful studies, controlling implementation precisely, give us information about how effective variations in these areas can be. And, as W. Edwards Deming (1982) has reminded businesses, the study of variance is important. Watching changes in the mean or median only loses the rich information to be found from inquiry into the range of effects.

Our committee finds some interesting information on what we call "the creation of chaos." In studying the research on change, they discover that many districts literally bombard, to use Michael Fullan's analogy, their schools and teachers with "paper" initiatives and "mandates" that far exceed the capacity to provide adequate support. Our folks begin to realize that only a few district initiatives can be pursued at one time and that faculties need to learn to work together to generate their own initiatives and to implement those strongly. (For more on formative evaluation and the regular assessment of effects, see David 1990; Joyce, Murphy, Showers, and Murphy 1989; Levine 1991; Sirotnik 1987; Slavin and Madden 1989.)

Preliminary Decisions of the Committee

Our committee makes several decisions that lead to the next phase of inquiry:

• To survey the field of tested curricular, instructional, and technological alternatives to lay a knowledge base for initiatives that are likely to pay off.

• To establish the principle that whatever avenues are chosen will be managed in such a way that changes in curriculum, instruction, and technology take place.

• To examine their current staff development programs and to revamp them, if necessary, to establish models that will increase the probability that their content, when chosen, will be implemented.

• To develop procedures to track implementation of innovations when they are chosen and document resulting student learning.

• To begin to involve everyone in the organization—teachers, building administrators, support personnel, and central office staff— in the study of school renewal.

The restructuring group wisely realizes that everyone must be engaged in the problem-solving process—that broad participation in decision making, training, implementation, and the study of effects will be part of their new organization. They also decide to prepare school faculties to take charge of a substantial portion of the decisions about direction. They will encourage the development of leadership teams and support them with appropriate training on collaborative decision making and the action research process.

The first phase has produced the realization that they need to revamp how they have conducted the business of maintaining and improving their organization. Relationships will change, and roles will blur. New and improved information systems and staff development systems will evolve. The power of school faculties to make and implement decisions will be enlarged. The committee, along with leadership teams, will regulate the number of district initiatives, doing fewer things more powerfully and balancing districtwide initiatives with approaches that school faculties vigorously pursue. This balancing act is difficult for them, for the members of our cross-role group are accustomed to going their autonomous ways. They are not accustomed to thrashing out just which *few* initiatives they will focus on (or maybe just *one* approach) during any one period of time.

Important Questions

In their last meeting in this first phase of their inquiry, committee members ask a series of important questions about the probability of keeping the focus on student learning central in the decision-making process:

• Can we expect to generate much higher levels of achievement than we now have?

• Can we virtually eliminate failure?

• Can the school effectively ameliorate the effects of impoverished backgrounds?

• Can all students become much more literate than at present?

• Can schools propel great numbers of students into levels of achievement rarely seen today?

• Are powerful options available, and is there evidence that they can make a difference?

The answers to all these questions are largely affirmative. The students of school improvement have built a little storehouse of successful options and, more important, learned how to get them implemented until they see differences in student learning (Walberg 1990; Bloom 1984; Madden et al. 1993; Joyce et al. 1992).

Thus, our committee members emerge from this phase of their work optimistic, although a little intimidated, for the realization is dawning that they are taking on something quite a bit larger than patching up the old schoolhouse. Their future will involve them in the formidable task of trying to create a changed organizational culture.

7

The District Restructuring Committee: Scene Two— Surveying Some General Options

OUR COMMITTEE GOES ON A RETREAT WITH THE NEWLY ELECTED leadership team members. Everyone puts forth ideas about what should be the priorities for changes that will increase student learning. The list is culled for redundancy, and they head off into the literature. They begin with the study of structural changes that can be made administratively, deferring the study of curricular and instructional options until their next phase. They are in for some surprises.

To a person, their chief surprise is that their collective common sense is not a completely reliable guide to what will work. Some popular innovations have had very weak or no effects; some have actually made things worse. The committee finds several such examples, including site-based school improvement, voucher programs, magnet schools, and the imposition of standards.

Site-Based School Improvement

They find that site-based school improvement efforts are far more difficult to manage than many people have assumed. There is also information about how to make it work. Both in the literature and in councils of policymakers, faculties are encouraged to study the school climate and the states of growth of the students and, based on the findings, to generate initiatives to improve the school.

Several studies have examined how school faculties respond to the challenge. Rosenholtz (1989) found that most faculties become "stuck" in the process, unable to agree on direction or to take action. David and Peterson (1984) studied efforts, some heavily funded, where volunteer schools were granted discretionary resources to engage in the process of self-renewal. They, too, found that most of those schools were also "stuck," in terms of effects on students, despite the grants. Most of those who were less stuck had not made initiatives in curriculum implementation or instruction, but had generated changes in scheduling, parent involvement, disciplinary codes, and other areas believed to be important but that did not require changes in what is taught or how it is taught.

Calhoun's studies (1991, 1992) of school faculties learning to engage in schoolwide action research indicate that nearly all schools need facilitation and technical assistance if they are to progress to unified action that affects instruction and student learning (see also David 1989; Sizer 1991; Timar 1989). For many schools, *extensive technical assistance* is needed if the "site-based" approach is to yield improved education for all students (Levine 1991, Levine and Lezotte 1990, Calhoun and Glickman 1993, Sizer 1984, Goodlad 1984). The reason sites need help is that the action research process depends on the development of norms of collegiality and the process of developing collective decision making; and collective action collides with the norms of privatism and autonomy that have for so long characterized the school workplace (Lortie 1975).

Voucher Plans

Various forms of the "voucher" have been touted by the federal government and have obtained support from many segments of the population. What is little known is that twenty years ago, the same government supported, at considerable cost, a series of projects to test the worth of various voucher plans. The results were indifferent in terms of student achievement. Perhaps more important, the evaluation tested one of the central theses of the voucher: that competition for students would cause schools to generate improvement efforts. Schools did *not* respond to the voucher by engaging in innovative activity to become more attractive to their clients. The evaluators concluded that if the government wanted innovation to occur, it should fund it directly rather than hoping that it would be a natural consequence of competition (see Cohen and Farrar 1977; Rand Corporation 1981; Raywid 1985, 1987; Cookson 1992).

Magnet Schools

Some other forms of "choice" programs, such as magnet high schools, have been of questionable value in improving the achievement of students admitted to them and, moreover, have been hurtful to students not admitted to them. Moore and Davenport's (1989) analysis of the effects of magnet school programs on the nonadmitted students indicates that, in the large eastern cities, they are a virtual social disaster.

Pressure Through Standards

Our restructuring committee also learns that several common ways of putting pressure on schools, such as increasing the intensity of testing programs and changing standards for promotion and graduation, do not appear to stimulate change or to have an effect on student learning. Instead, some of these tactics to improve "quality" have actually increased retentions and numbers of dropouts (Gamoran and Berends 1987; Oakes 1985; Potter and Wall 1992; Slavin and Madden 1989).

℀   ℀   ℀

Our committee finds that these "indirect" approaches to school improvement have not worked very well, despite their common-sense appeal, and have had some unpleasant side effects.

The restructuring committee decides to focus most of their energy on direct approaches for increasing student learning and collegial energy: They will create initiatives in curriculum and instruction one at a time and conduct each initiative so that it builds the capacity for collective action within each school and across the district. The question now becomes one of selecting promising initiatives. There-fore, the next task is to assess the sizes of effects to be gained from various innovations in curriculum and instruction. Although some teachers have been involved in the first two phases, all teachers will play important roles in phase three. Thus, the leadership teams help each school faculty organize itself into study groups that will be involved in the next phases of inquiry.

8

The District Restructuring Committee: Scene Three— Surveying Curricular and Instructional Initiatives

THE RESTRUCTURING COMMITTEE MOVES BEYOND "STRUCTURAL" initiatives and generates a long list of curricular and instructional approaches. Each study group selects one initiative and proceeds to examine the research undergirding it. Study group members conduct a meta-analysis of the literature connected to their initiatives. They are hunting for the size of effects (Glass 1982) to be expected if the approach they are studying were to be adopted by a school or the district as a whole. Pure statistical significance is not enough. Two options directed toward the same objective might each accomplish significant effects, but the magnitude of results from one might be five times more effective with students than the effect of another. For example, various cooperative learning strategies have quite different magnitudes of academic effects, whereas all appear to help social skills and self-esteem (Rolheiser-Bennett 1986). The catch is that a *good implementation is required.*

As a preliminary activity to facilitate the work of each study group, members of the leadership team in each school present and lead discussions on the concept of "effect size." A basic understanding of effect size will help our groups sort out the options.

The Concept of "Effect Size"

To estimate the size of effects of an educational procedure requires that there be a set of studies relevant to that procedure. Optimally, these studies would be controlled experiments in which the investigators took measures of the students at the beginning, assigned the students to control and experimental groups on the basis of pretests, exposed the groups to the procedures, and measured again at the end of the treatment and possibly at intervals thereafter, comparing the distribution of scores of the two groups in terms of means and standard deviations. The "effect size" statistic (Glass 1982) is then computed. By repeatedly computing the sizes of differences in effects with each study that is conducted, we can arrive at a reasonable picture of the relative effectiveness of various teaching and curricular procedures.

To help the study groups understand the concept of effect size and how it works, the leadership teams review several concepts that enable us to describe and compare scores on various measures. For example, we describe distributions of scores in terms of *central tendencies*, which refer to the clustering of scores around the middle of the distribution, and to *variance*, or the dispersion of these scores.

Terms describing central tendency include the *average* or arithmetic mean, which is computed by summing the scores and dividing by the number of scores; the *median* or middle score, in which half the scores are above and half are below the median score; and the *mode*, which is the most frequent score in the distribution and, graphically, the highest point in the distribution. In Figure 8.1, which the teams present to the study groups, the average, the median, and the mode are all in the same place because the distribution is completely symmetrical.

The *dispersion of scores* in a distribution is described in terms of the *range*, the distance between the highest and lowest scores; the *rank*, frequently described in *percentile* (e.g., the 20th score from the top in a 100-person distribution is at the 80th percentile because 20 percent of the scores are above and 80 percent are below it); and the *standard deviation*, which describes how widely or narrowly scores are distributed. This overview of how to describe a distribution is an important part of helping our study groups develop an understanding of how analyzing effects works.

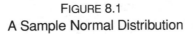

FIGURE 8.1
A Sample Normal Distribution

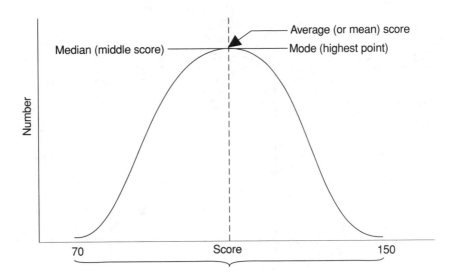

Source: Joyce, B., M. Weil, and B. Showers. (1992). *Models of Teaching* (4th ed., pp. 20–24). Boston: Allyn and Bacon.

The teams explain that standard deviation describes the position of a score in relation to the *mean* of a continuum of scores, and effect size describes the *differences between means* of procedures as a proportion of standard deviation. They continue with an example. The teams use a transparency based on Figure 8.2 to illustrate.

In Figure 8.2, the range is from 70 (the lowest score) to 150 (the highest score). The 50th percentile score is at the middle (in this case, corresponding with the average, the mode, and the median). Standard deviations are marked off by the vertical lines labeled +1 *SD*, +2 *SD*, and so on. Note that the percentile rank of the score one standard deviation above the mean is 84 (84 percent of the scores are below that point); the rank two standard deviations above the mean is 97; and three standard deviations above the mean is 99.

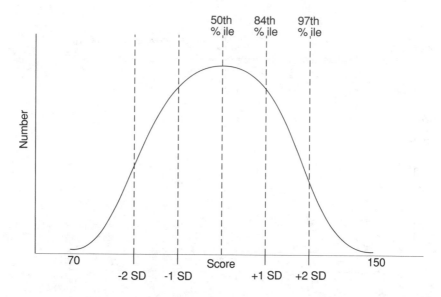

FIGURE 8.2

Dispersion of Scores in a Normal Distribution

Source: Joyce, B., M. Weil, and B. Showers. (1992). *Models of Teaching* (4th ed., pp. 20–24). Boston: Allyn and Bacon.

When the mean, median, and mode coincide, as in Figure 8.2, and the distribution of scores is as symmetrical as the ones depicted in these figures, the distribution is referred to as *normal*. The concept of normal distributions is very useful in statistical operations, although many actual distributions are not symmetrical, as we will see. However, to explain the concept of effect size, the teams use symmetrical, "normal" distributions.

The Effects of a Complex Cooperative-Learning Model of Teaching

Continuing their presentation on effect size, the members of the leadership teams lead a review of a careful study of a complex model of teaching. They use a recent study of student learning through Group Investigation, an intensive instructional approach that combines elaborate methods for collaborative activity with scientific methods of inquiry. In this study, Shlomo Sharan and Hana Shachar (1988) illustrate how rapidly students can accelerate their learning rates. Their study focuses on a problem that exists in many societies—that students whose families are regarded as socially and economically disadvantaged frequently display low achievement and receive disadvantaging treatment in the classroom from other students and from teachers. Sharan and Shachar prepared social studies teachers to organize their students into learning communities and compared the classroom interaction and academic achievement with classes taught by the customary "whole class" method. In Israel, where the study was conducted, students of Middle-Eastern origin generally belong to the "disadvantaged" population, whereas students of European origin generally are more advantaged. In this study, students from both origins were mixed in classes. The research design compared the achievement of the students who were taught using Group Investigation with students taught by the "whole class" method most common in Israeli schools. Figure 8.3 presents the results for the students of Middle-Eastern origin under the two conditions.

FIGURE 8.3

Comparison of Achievement of Middle-Eastern Students
in Group-Investigation and "Whole-Class" Conditions

		Group Investigation ($N = 47$)	Whole Class ($N = 26$)
History pretest			
	Mean	14.81	12.31
	SD	7.20	7.05
History post-test			
	Mean	50.17	27.23
	SD	14.44	13.73
Mean gain		35.36	14.92

The Group-Investigation-taught, Middle-Eastern-origin students achieved average gains nearly two and a half times those of their whole-class counterparts. These normally disadvantaged students also achieved larger gains than did the European-origin students taught by the more typical whole-class method (35.16 to 21.05) and exceeded them on the post-test. In other words, the "socially disadvantaged" students taught with Group Investigation learned at rates above those of the "socially advantaged" students taught by teachers who did not have the repertoire provided by Group Investigation. The model had enabled them to become more powerful students immediately. The average gain by the Western-origin students was *twice* that of their "whole-class" counterparts. Thus, the treatment was effective for students from both backgrounds.

Let's see what the results look like in "effect size" terms. Figure 8.4 compares the post-test scores of the low-socioeconomic-status (SES) students in the control group (whole-class) and Group Investigation treatments. The average score of the Group Investigation treatment corresponds to about the 92nd percentile of the distribution of the whole-class students. The effect size is computed by dividing the difference between the two means by the standard deviation of the control, or whole-class, group. The effect size in this case is 1.6 standard deviations, using the formula

$$ES = \frac{\text{Average of experimental group} - \text{Average of control}}{\text{Standard deviation of control}}$$

Thus, the average of the Group-Investigation-taught students was about one and a half standard deviations above the average of the whole-class-taught students.

Sharan and Shachar's study combined three elements: a powerful model of instruction, enough staff development to help teachers learn how to use the method, and the actual use of Group Investigation in the classroom. The teams noted that in this study, curriculum content was not changed; yet learning rates were accelerated rapidly by innovation in instruction.

FIGURE 8.4
A Sample Depiction of Effect Size:
The Sharon and Shachar (1988) Study

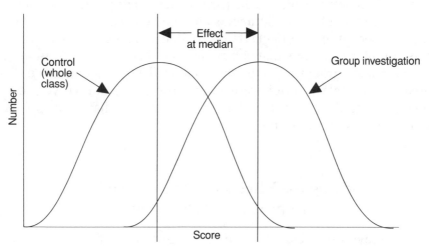

Source: Joyce, B., M. Weil, and B. Showers. (1992). *Models of Teaching* (4th ed., pp. 20–24). Boston: Allyn and Bacon.

Using Syntheses of Research

By accumulating the findings from many studies, we can discern the consistency of effects of teaching and curriculum patterns, as well as their average effects. We can also explore variations within curriculum areas. The teams use the example of Hillock's (1987) review of the effects of various approaches to the teaching of writing. To the surprise of our study groups, they learn from Hillock's review that the formal study of grammar and mechanics by itself has virtually no effect at all on quality of writing (in studies conducted as far back as 100 years!). Modeling of writing devices has an average effect size of about .22, with "sentence combining" at .35 from the intermediate grades on. The highest effect size (.57) was from well-implemented "inquiry" approaches to the teaching of writing. The inquiry approaches require more staff development for a good implementation.

Learning about the need for staff development helped the faculties grapple with the relationships among curriculum implementation, staff development, and the focus of school improvement energy when the more effective strategies are selected. The teams conclude their presentations on effect size by emphasizing the need to consider this complex of factors that contribute to a successful innovation.

Our study groups dig in to the research. They concentrate on two areas: large-scale school improvement programs that involve everyone in a school or district, and teaching strategies that have applications across age levels and subject areas.

Studying the Effects of Large-Scale School Improvement Programs

In a few instances, intensive, multiple-school efforts have been made and evaluated to the extent that the results can be clearly perceived. Our study groups have a great time with their literature, for all the large-scale programs combined a number of changes in their overall strategies. These are some of the things they discover and discuss.

Combining Curriculum, Instruction, and Tutoring

The Center for Research on Effective Schooling for Disadvantaged Students at Johns Hopkins University (Slavin, Madden, Karweit, Livermon, and Dolan 1990) is beginning to report its efforts to improve primary education in the Baltimore schools. The Success for All program is a complex initiative that combines an intensive reading curriculum with close-order diagnosis of learning problems, immediate intervention with tutoring aimed directly at the problems, cooperative learning, and family support teams. The staff development program is spread throughout the year, with heavy emphasis on follow-up for implementation. The focus is on preventing the onset of the downward spiral that so often begins during the primary years and leaves the students unable to cope with the ordinary demands of the upper grades. While the program is expected to have its largest effects cumulatively over time, the product of the first year is achievement that is normal for the nation, rather than the dismal picture that generally ensues. (The program developers aim at bringing *all* students to satisfactory levels and not accepting the losses that occur when normally distributed achievement occurs.) It is interesting that the largest effects from the first-year program occurred in the third grade, leading to optimism about what can be done with the somewhat more mature learners who have accumulated learning deficits from the earlier grades.

The multiyear effects of the program are very positive. Retention has been reduced greatly (from about 10 percent to 1–3 percent in the project schools). Gains in reading are considerable across a variety of tests, and fewer students are qualifying for special education services because their achievement is satisfactory (Madden, Slavin, Karweit, Dolan, and Wasik 1991).

The complex Success for All intervention is reminiscent of Spaulding's (1970) program for a similar population in North Carolina. Spaulding's most important academic goal was to raise aptitude to learn as measured by tests of ability or intelligence. He also used a combination of careful diagnosis, direct and immediate intervention, intensive reading instruction, and several well-tested models of teaching, including social learning theory, simulations, role-playing, and cooperative study. The ability indexes of the average student in Spaulding's initiative rose about a third of a standard deviation after three years. As in the case of Success for All, the results indicate that curriculum and instruction can be aimed directly at learning capacity.

Using Intensive, Instruction-Oriented Staff Development

In Pittsburgh, a side effect of the development of an extensive districtwide staff development program was a test of what can happen if some of the most highly regarded teachers in a large district are concentrated in a high school whose lower SES population has been far below the national average. The Schenley School became a staff development center where outstanding teachers were brought together. Other district teachers rotated into the school, spending several weeks observing those teachers and studying instruction (Wallace, Lemahieu, and Bickel 1990). There was an immediate rise in standardized test scores in eight of nine curriculum areas. In terms of the percentage of students scoring at or above the national average, the rise in total language results was from 27 to 61 percent, in reading from 28 to 45 percent, in physical science from 21 to 63 percent, in biology from 13 to 41 percent, and in algebra from 29 to 73 percent. The gains were maintained or increased during the second year. Not only were these large sizes of improvements, but they were also immediate.

High schools need not feel hopeless about students with poor learning histories. The gifted Schenley teachers, working in an environment that intensified the study of instruction, "jacked up" the learning environment of their school immediately. The students responded by allowing their intelligence to become focused on eliminating their deficits and, in the main, looking more able at graduation than many of their counterparts who had not suffered cumulative deficits in their past education.

Combining Collaborative Organization with Intensive Staff Development on Several Models of Teaching

The Richmond County, Georgia, School Improvement Program focused on instruction, staff development, and organizing faculties for collaborative action. Schools entered the program as units. To participate, 80 percent of each faculty had to vote to participate. Within the program, all teachers in each participating school studied a set of well-proven models of teaching selected to increase the learning capacity of their students. The faculties were organized into study groups and elected councils whose responsibility was to examine information about the health of the school and plan school improvement initiatives (Joyce, Murphy, Showers, and Murphy 1989).

In some schools, the need for school improvement was urgent. In one of the middle schools, for example, the students had such poor histories of learning that only 30 percent of them achieved promotion at the end of the year before the project began. Scores on standard tests revealed that the average student in the school had gained only about six months' achievement for each year in school. (Ten months is the national average.) The school district had made a number of initiatives to alleviate the situation, including special programs for "at risk" students, lowering class size and increasing counseling services, all with little effect. However, as the teachers learned to use models designed to increase cooperative activity, teach concepts, and help students learn to work inductively and memorize information, student learning rates began to improve dramatically. By the end of the first year, 70 percent of the students in the middle school achieved the standards required for promotion; and 95 percent achieved promotion at the end of the second year. Judging from the standardized tests administered at the end of the second year, the average students in the school were achieving at a normal rate, that is, gaining ten months of learning for ten months of effort, when compared to the United States population as a whole. Time lost in disciplinary action decreased dramatically, to about one-fifth of the amount lost before the program began.

Of course, it is unlikely that any one intervention could have achieved effects of this magnitude; but the combination of initiatives helped the students learn a variety of strategies that enabled them to educate themselves more strongly. The increased collegiality in the faculty also contributed to the development of a more positive social climate and a general increase of energy in the school.

Studying Curriculum and Social Climate, with Community Involvement

Another program was a curriculum initiative that emphasized the social climate of the school. In the Panama Region of the Department of Defense Dependents Schools' initiative, Operation Just Read and Write, the staff studied how much the average student was reading independent of school assignments. Throughout the initiative, whereby all of the schools and the district central office promoted at-home independent reading with extensive parent involvement, reading and writing quantity and quality were studied. The 5th grade data illustrate the changes that were typical in all the schools and at all grade levels. Before the project began, the average 5th grade student read about seven books per year out of school, a figure considerably above the U.S. average. In the second year of the project, the average 5th grade student read 59 books during the school year, an eight-fold increase. The lowest number of titles recorded was three times the average recorded as baseline when the program was initiated. The average 1st grade student read 175 books during the second year of the project, compared to 50 during the baseline period.

Although not every initiative could hope to be as successful as Operation Just Read and Write, its findings helped the study groups grasp the magnitude of change in student behavior that could result from a well-articulated school improvement effort.

Characteristics of Effective Large-Scale School Improvement Initiatives

Although making large differences in student achievement through school improvement programs is hardly routine, the number of reports and variety of programs having considerable success suggest that the technology for making rapid and significant change exists. The initiatives mentioned in this chapter are just a few of those our study groups discover. Effective implementation of "Mastery Learning" programs (Block and Anderson 1975, Bloom 1984) and Distar (Becker 1977) have generated some very impressive results, as have some applications of technology, including broadcast television development such as the products of the Children's Television Workshop (Ball and Bogatz 1970).

The programs described here share several characteristics:

• All have focused on specific student-learning goals. None had only general goals, such as "to make test scores go up."

• All have employed procedures tailored to their goals and backed by rationales grounded in theory or research or a combination of these.

• All have measured learning outcomes on a formative and summative basis, collecting information about student gains on a regular basis and not leaving evaluation to a yearly examination of post hoc information derived from standardized tests only.

• All have provided substantial amounts of staff development, in recognition that the initiative involved teacher and student learning of new procedures. The staff development targeted the content of the initiatives specifically. Researchers regularly collected data on the progress of implementation and made these results available to project personnel.

Studying the Effects of Teaching Strategies

Several study groups discover that several instructional procedures can generate powerful effects. They hunt for strategies that have promising content for instructional initiatives relevant to the curriculum of their district. They find evidence of strong effects on student learning for various lines of study, such as science, the organization of materials for presentations, the development of problem-solving skills, and mastery of specific content. Many of the teaching strategies that have student effects generate or release skills for thinking effectively.

Research on the implementation of "scientific-inquiry" teaching strategies reveals an interesting pattern to our group. These inductive models were designed to teach students the methods of science. That was and is their primary, direct mission. Research clearly indicates that those models achieve those effects very well (Bredderman 1983; El Nemr 1979). Also, good implementation of scientific inquiry strategies increases the amount of information students learn, encourages their development of concepts, and improves their attitudes toward science. These models also enhance students' ability to learn—exposure to inductive methods apparently increases aptitude to approach learning tasks independently.

Some teaching strategies have achieved small but consistent effects that accumulate over time. The Advance Organizer Model (Ausubel 1960) was designed to increase the acquisition and retention of information from lectures and other kinds of presentations— such as films and readings. It achieves its modest results consistently ($ES = 0.20$) when the "organizers" are properly used (Joyce and Showers 1988). However, lectures, written assignments, films, and other media are so pervasive as educational tools that even relatively modest increments of knowledge from specific uses of organizers can add up to impressive increases in learning.

A few models of learning have dramatic effects in specific applications. The "link-word" method, one of several models that assist memorization, has increased rates of learning two to three times in a series of experiments. Students learned given amounts of material two to three times more rapidly when they used the link-word methods than they would have if they had used customary procedures for memorizing words (Pressley, Levin, and Delaney 1982). Effect sizes of about 1.00 are more common, however. The model is applicable to higher-order goals, such as teaching hierarchies of concepts in science (Levin and Levin 1990), addressing one of the important and most complex instructional goals in curriculum.

Our study groups also begin to realize that sometimes the objective is to virtually eliminate dispersion in a distribution. For example, instructors of pilots wish to teach so effectively that *no one* crashes during training and, even better, that everyone learns to fly. Driver education has parallel objectives. Some instructional objectives need to focus on certain objectives for all students, such as ensuring that *all* students learn to read and can write serviceable prose, are knowledgeable about citizenship and how to participate effectively in the society, and so on. Educators who think from this point of view can generate intensive instructional initiatives and conduct informal studies that determine if they are able to achieve "total" effects like these. A teacher colleague of ours used mnemonic devices to teach his 4th grade students the names of the states and their capitals. *All* his students learned all of them and remembered them throughout the year. Thus the distribution of his class's scores on tests of their ability to supply all the names on a blank map had no range at all. The average score was the top possible score. There were no percentile ranks because the students' scores were all tied at the top. For some objectives—basic knowledge about the Constitution of the United States, computation skills, a basic reading vocabulary—we want, in fact, to have a very high degree of success for all our students because anything less is terribly disadvantaging for them.

Thus, as our groups study the teaching strategies that have a historical record of yielding student effects, they find no easy route that is superior for all purposes, or even that should be the sole avenue to any given objective. However, they do find powerful options that can be linked to the multiple educational goals that constitute a complete educational diet. The message is that the most effective teachers (and designers of instruction and curriculum) need to master a range of teaching models and prepare for a career-long process of adding new strategies and strengthening their old ones.

As the study groups report to one another, they agree that there is good information out there, more than enough to sustain initiatives for some time to come, but no panaceas.

9

The District Restructuring Committee: Scene Four— Involving the Community

ANOTHER IMPORTANT PROCESS BEGINS AS OUR STUDY GROUPS share the results of their collective inquiry. Policymakers and the school faculties must now select initiatives from a large storehouse of options, and they have to deal with the problem of change in a new way. Whatever they begin will require change at all levels of the system.

Where Now for the Self-Renewing Organization?

Our district is organized for action and has a reasonable chance of re-creating itself into a self-renewing organization through collective study. Nearly everyone has helped open the storehouse of effective instructional and curricular procedures, and they are ready to choose more powerful options for school renewal. They will work together through improved staff development using collective action. We believe they will succeed in creating a more vital workplace for themselves and a more powerful educational environment for their students. As a social unit, these individuals have taken the trouble to find out what works and what it takes to make things happen. They will make a good run at creating a self-renewing organization. What role should the community play in the process?

We have concentrated thus far on what educators can do to make common cause. However, we believe that ever more powerful and rapid change occurs when the community of educators brings parents and other community members into central roles in the process.

Involvement of the community generates energy and creativity. The process becomes more complex, but more vital as well.

The Client and the Organization

Parents enroll their children in the organization (the school) to ensure cultural participation at the highest level. These clients do not come to the individual teacher; they come to the district and school as educational organizations. *For their tenure with us, we want to make parents part of our learning community*, enlisting their energies in our part of the growth and socialization of their children. We need to see ourselves as an organization that serves them as a part of the aspirations of each individual and of society, for that is how they see us. As individuals, educators are part of an institution set up to serve the young. As individuals, parents become part of the educational organization—not just partners with, but part of it—and we work with them, bringing their strength and skill to bear on the collective task of educating children.

Given the vital relationships among students, teachers, and the organization and the legal position of boards of education in the school district, research on the involvement of community members in the school improvement process is remarkably scarce. To be sure, there is a sizable literature on the importance of the general involvement of the client in organizations that serve them (see, e.g., Comer 1987, Lewin 1948, Gardner 1963). The conclusion of that literature is that *client-serving institutions are much more successful when they blur the distinctions between the professional and lay community and involve the client wherever possible in the functions of the organization.* Some notable recent efforts have built avenues for increasing parent involvement in both in- and out-of-school functions; and many categorical programs, particularly those in special education, have involved parents as individuals in the development of the structure of educational programs for their children.

Lessons from the Urban-Rural School Development Program

The Urban-Rural School Development Program was designed to yield information about how to structure parent and community involvement in the general school renewal process (Joyce 1977). This large-scale effort demonstrates how effective intensive involvement of community members can be. In this program, twenty-six Urban-Rural projects (all in underachieving schools in economically poor communities, half of them rural, half urban) were operated at the school level, with approval and support from the district office and the board of education. Each school maintained a school-community council, in which elected community members had a majority of one over elected teachers. The council was to oversee the health of the school, make initiatives for school improvement, develop the necessary staff development to support the initiatives, assess the effects, and go on to make further initiatives. Community members were involved at all stages, helping examine the health of the school, selecting problems to focus on, communicating with parents, lending a hand when possible, and generally making common cause with the educators. The thesis was that the educator-client collaboration would generate energy for school improvement initiatives.

The general evaluation of the Urban-Rural program addressed several questions important to us here (Joyce 1977). First, concerning the relationships between the teachers and community members on the council—did they achieve parity in participation in decision making, and how effectively did they organize the community in general? The results were positive. The councils developed high degrees of integration. An interesting sidelight was how the roles of community member and teacher blurred in the process. Observers were frequently unable to distinguish the two roles during council discussions.

Second, were the efforts productive in terms of school improvement? The evaluation indicated that all the sites generated far more school-improvement activity than the average school does without parent involvement; and it greatly surpassed some programs, such as the California School Improvement Programs, which were heavily funded but generated a much lower level of community involvement (Berman and Gjelten 1983). Much more staff development was generated to support the initiatives. *The greater the community involvement, and the more that process parity was achieved in the sites, the greater the school improvement activities.* Also, most initiatives were implemented—a far higher proportion than are usually followed through in the average site-based school improvement program. The integrated educator/community organization "saw things through" and coped with anxieties and discouragements far better than the average faculty does, working alone. In addition, much community energy was generated in relation to the school, ranging from help in organizing events to widespread involvement of volunteer aides.

The results of the Urban-Rural process, as do the results of the Operation Just Read and Write program described earlier, support the thesis that extensive community involvement increases productivity in school improvement, as well as having the obvious benefits of enlisting parents and other community members in roles important to the school. The more people involved, the more energy available to support desirable changes.

ℛ   ℛ   ℛ

Our district begins to add community members to the leadership teams and induces them to form study groups of parents and other adults to become part of the process of building the self-renewing organization.

10 Moral Resolve and Technical Knowledge

THE FABRIC OF SCHOOLING IS CUT FROM MORAL CLOTH. THE CON-sequences of either rich or impoverished education are matters of cultural wealth or privation. The technical-professional processes for creating self-renewing organizations are not analogous to the dispassionate engineering of material objects. Education is life. The stubborn resolve to perfect our society and provide a better life for our children provides us the reasons to examine the health of our schools and search for ways to improve them. Technical knowledge influences resolve by providing an understanding that schools *can* be much better than they are. But a passion for life bubbles at the core of the venture to renew education.

Made by us—the present generation of parents and teachers—the process of schooling needs to create the opportunity for our children to exceed us, collectively and individually. Through education, we hope to seed the conditions for a society in which all citizens participate fully economically and politically and whose intellectual life is rich and full. Otherwise our educational system will perpetuate the defects of our society as it transmits its virtues. For example, it will perpetuate social inequities unless it prepares citizens to remedy them (see Apple 1989 for a thorough discussion). The challenging question posed in 1932 by George Counts, "Dare the schools improve the social order?" is as fresh today as when it was written.

Urgent Contemporary Requirements

Probably because of our history of local creation and control of schools, which has many virtues, we parents and educators tend to see schooling in terms of meeting the needs of our particular community and the characteristics of our children, which is good. However, we are members of a large and diverse society whose changing character has to be addressed by each school. Also, the education of all our children needs to prepare them for life in our rapidly evolving national and international society.

The following are just a few of the urgent contemporary requirements of education. These can remind us of the richness of the avenues we can pursue in our quest.

Literacy in the Largest Sense Is Basic.

There are two fundamental types of literacy. Literacy includes knowledge of the written, visual, and enactive storehouse of the world—the *big* library of books, plays, films, music, and scientific knowledge—as described in Philip Phenix' (1964) *Realms of Meaning*. Knowing what is out there and how to access it—the structures of the storehouses of knowledge—is essential.

The swirling realities of the cultures of the world, the searches of the world's societies for meaning and resources, the real stuff of life on this planet, form the second essential type of literacy. Although we have sympathy for the kinds of knowledge advocated by some popular critics (e.g., Finn 1991, Hirsch 1987), the grasp of the riches of the heritage and the fabulous countryside of contemporary life far override any bit of knowledge for importance in the lives of our children. We must reconceptualize classic education (Sizer 1984, Adler 1982, Goodlad 1984).

Without an educated perspective, the pressing needs of society can be dealt with on an overly pragmatic basis, and the major current needs will be trivialized.

Equity Is Critical.

Well over a million U.S. students are dropping out of school each year; another million or so are graduating with knowledge and skills that are marginal for economic survival. Neither from the perspective of these people as individuals nor from the perspective of the health of the society can we tolerate this statistic; it is morally imperative that we change the condition. From a technical perspective, the means exist to educate all students well and must be used to change this condition. Whether we continue to replicate and extend our ghettoes is a matter of choice. The creation of equity is not just a matter of improving inner-city schools. It is a matter of orienting all our young citizens to the moral necessity of creating a society where all citizens work continuously to improve the lot of everyone.

Tending the Reservoir of Human Talent Is Vitally Important.

We need to consider both the quality of the substance of education and the orientation toward productive life. For example, the proportion of American students who are entering our graduate schools in highly technical subjects is diminishing in relation to students from other countries. One cause of this shortage is that so few of our students engage in the advanced study of the sciences. Partly this is because they have not been prepared substantively to do so. Partly it is because they have not been oriented toward productive intellectual life. And we have greatly underestimated the number of people who can become highly educated.

Basic Knowledge About the World Is Essential.

What should be routine accomplishments in basic education for all students—global literacy, the development of personal reading habits, the ability to write clear and well-organized prose—are achieved only partially for most students and not at all for a significant number. From the moral perspective, we must let *no* students fail. Technically speaking, we have another area of choice: the means exist, and we have only to use them.

Routine Use of Contemporary Technology Should Become Just That—Routine.

Schools are gradually learning to incorporate computers and other electronically based technologies, but the emphasis is on the qualifier *gradual*. Schools need to be places where students reach toward the front edges of technology, rather than places that slowly catch up to changes already embedded in the "best use" segments of the social system. Here is an area where knowledge about curriculum and instruction has exceeded knowledge about how to restructure the school environment.

*A Planetary View of Personal and
Social Life Is Necessary.*

A global worldview is needed not only because it connects us to our neighbors, but because management of future life will require it. The evolving international society is resulting in a dramatically changed ecology; and the biocultural, macroeconomic, and political systems are changing rapidly and will affect everyone. As the world population moves from five to six billion in the 1990s, the "third" world becomes a full participant in economic and political affairs. As the balance of influence and possibilities of multicultural experience change, planetary perspectives will become essential for personal and societal health (Tye 1991).

Need for Substantial Reform

To meet these needs requires strenuous efforts to bring about substantial changes in education. Small or cosmetic changes will not suffice. The demands of the emerging world society will outreach our most successful students, and the social tragedies of our inner cities will deepen unless we substantially reform the ways we conduct education.

Currently, educators, government agencies, and citizens' committees are acknowledging these areas as priorities for change by generating a new era of intensive initiatives to try to increase the quantity and quality of student learning. The beginning points of these efforts vary considerably, as we can see from the various uses of the term *restructuring* in the current literature about school improvement (Elmore 1990, Joyce 1991). Restructuring initiatives, however, all address a number of problems that are important in the society as a whole. *Moral purpose should drive the efforts.* However, the technical tasks of sorting out initiatives from various sources are formidable. The overall challenge of developing a self-renewing organization is the largest one for us at present. We have to supersede our past history of approaching problems on an ad hoc basis by creating an educational culture that will be simultaneously better for us and for our students.

Bibliography

Adler, M.J. (1982). *The Paideia Proposal: An Educational Manifesto*. New York: Macmillan.

Apple, M. (1989). *Ideology and Curriculum*. London: Routledge and Kegan Paul.

Argyris, C., and E. Schön. (1974). *Theory into Practice: Increasing Professional Effectiveness*. San Francisco: Jossey-Bass.

Ausubel, D. (1960). "The Use of Advanced Organizers in the Learning and Retention of Meaningful Verbal Material." *Journal of Educational Psychology* 51: 267–272.

Baker, R.G. (1983). "The Contribution of Coaching to Transfer of Training." Doctoral diss., University of Oregon, Eugene.

Baldridge, V., and T. Deal. (1983). *The Dynamics of Organizational Change in Education*. Boston: Addison-Wesley.

Ball, S., and G.A. Bogatz. (1970). *The First Year of Sesame Street*. Princeton, N.J.: Educational Testing Service.

Barth, R.S. (1991a). *Improving Schools from Within*. San Francisco: Jossey-Bass.

Barth, R.S. (October 1991b). "Restructuring Schools: Some Questions for Teachers and Principals." *Phi Delta Kappan* 73, 2: 123–128.

Becker, W. (1977). "Teaching Reading and Writing to the Disadvantaged—What We Have Learned from Field Research." *Harvard Educational Review* 47, 3: 518–543.

Bellack, A. (1963). *The Language of the Classroom*. New York: Teachers College Press.

Bennett, B. (1987). *The Effectiveness of Staff Development Training Practices: A Meta-Analysis*. Doctoral diss., University of Oregon, Eugene.

Bennis, W.G. (1989). *Why Leaders Can't Lead*. San Francisco: Jossey-Bass.

Berman, P., and T. Gjelten. (1983). *Improving School Improvement*. Berkeley, Calif.: Weiler Associates.

Berman, P., and M. McLaughlin. (1975). *Federal Programs Supporting Educational Change*. Santa Monica, Calif.: Rand.

Block, J.W., and L.W. Anderson. (1975). *Mastery Learning in Classrooms*. New York: Macmillan.

Bloom, B.S. (1984). "The 2 Sigma Problem: The Search for Group Instruction as Effective as One-to-One Tutoring." *Educational Researcher* 13, 3: 4–16.

Blum, R.E., and A.W. Kneidek. (1991). "Strategic Improvement that Focuses on Student Achievement." *Educational Leadership* 48, 7: 17–21.

Bolam, R. (1990). "Recent Developments in England and Wales." In *Changing School Culture Through Staff Development*, edited by B. Joyce. 1990 ASCD Yearbook. Alexandria, Va.: ASCD.

Borg, W.R., W. Kallenbach, M. Morris, and A. Friebel. (1969). "Videotape Feedback and Microteaching in a Teacher Training Model." *Journal of Experimental Education* 37, 22: 9–16.

Bossert, S., D. Dwyer, B. Rowan, and G. Lee. (1982). "The Instructional Management Role of the Principal." *Educational Administration Quarterly* 18, 3: 34–64.

Bradford, L.P., J.R. Gibb, and K.D. Benne, eds. (1964). *T-Group Theory and Laboratory Method.* New York: Wiley.

Bredderman, T. (1983). "Effects of Activity-Based Elementary Science on Student Outcomes: A Quantitative Synthesis." *Review of Educational Research* 53, 4: 499–518.

Brookover, W. (1978). "Elementary School Social Climate and Student Achievement." *American Educational Research Journal* 15, 2: 301–318.

Brophy, J. (1992). "Probing the Subtleties of Subject-Matter Teaching." *Educational Leadership* 49, 7: 4–8.

Calhoun, E.F. (1991). "A Wide-Angle Lens: How to Increase the Variety, Collection, and Use of Data for School Improvement." Paper presented at the annual meeting of the American Educational Research Association, Chicago.

Calhoun, E.F. (1992). "A Status Report on Action Research in the League of Professional Schools." Paper presented at the annual meeting of the American Educational Research Association, San Francisco.

Calhoun, E.F., and C.D. Glickman. (1993). "Issues and Dilemmas of Action Research in the League of Professional Schools." Paper presented at the annual meeting of the American Educational Research Association, Atlanta.

Cochran-Smith, M. (1991). "Word Processing and Writing in Elementary Classrooms: A Critical Review of Related Literature." *Review of Educational Research* 61, 1: 107–155.

Cohen, D.K., and E. Farrar. (1977). "Power to the Parents? The Story of Education Vouchers." ERIC document number EJ165190.

Coleman, P., and L. LaRocque. (1990). *Struggling to Be "Good Enough" : Administrative Practices and School District Ethos.* New York: Falmer Press.

Comer, J. (1987). "New Haven's School-Community Connection." *Educational Leadership* 44, 6: 13–16.

Cookson, P.W., Jr., ed. (1992). *The Choice Controversy.* Newbury Park, Calif.: Corwin Press.

Corbett, H.D., and B.L. Wilson. (1991). *The Central Office Role in Instructional Improvement.* Philadelphia: Research for Better Schools.

Corey, S.M. (1953). *Action Research to Improve School Practices.* New York: Teachers College Press.

Counts, G. (1932). *Dare the School Build a New Social Order?* New York: The John Day Company.

Crandall, D., S. Loucks, M. Huberman, and M. Miles. (1982). *People, Policies, and Practices: Examining the Chain of School Improvement*, Vols. 1–10. Andover, Mass.: The Network.

Cuban, L. (1990). "Reforming Again, Again, and Again." *Educational Researcher* 19, 1: 3–13.

David, J.L. (1989). *Restructuring in Progress: Lessons from Pioneering Districts.* Washington, D.C.: National Governors' Association.

David, J.L. (1990). "Restructuring: Increased Autonomy and Changing Roles." Invited address presented at the annual meeting of the American Educational Research Association, Boston.

David, J., and S. Peterson. (1984). *Can Schools Improve Themselves? A Study of School-Based Improvement Programs*. Palo Alto, Calif.: Bay Area Research Group.

Davies, D. (1990). *Community Involvement*. Boston: Boston University.

Deal, T.E., and A.A. Kennedy. (1984). *Corporate Cultures: The Rites and Rituals of Cooperate Life*. Reading, Mass.: Addison-Wesley.

Deming, W.E. (1982). *Out of the Crisis*. Cambridge: Massachusetts Institute of Technology, Center for Advanced Engineering Study.

Dillon-Peterson, E. (1981). *Staff Development/Organizational Development*. 1981 ASCD Yearbook. Alexandria, Va.: ASCD.

Dole, J.A., G.G. Duffy, L.R. Roehler, and P.D. Pearson. (1991). "Moving from the Old to the New: Research on Reading Comprehension Instruction." *Review of Educational Research* 61, 2: 239–264.

Drucker, P.F. (1985). *Innovation and Entrepreneurship: Practice and Principles*. New York: Harper and Row.

Eisner, E. (1991). "What Really Counts in Schools." *Educational Leadership* 48, 5: 10–17.

Eisner, E., and E. Vallance, eds. (1974). *Conflicting Conceptions of Curriculum*. Berkeley, Calif.: McCutcheon.

El-Nemr, M.A. (1979). "Meta-Analysis of the Outcomes of Teaching Biology as Inquiry." Doctoral diss., University of Colorado, Boulder.

Elmore, R.F. (1990). "On Changing the Structure of Public Schools." In *Restructuring Schools*, edited by R.F. Elmore. San Francisco: Jossey-Bass.

Elmore, R.F. (1991a). *Innovation in Education Policy*. Durham, N.C.: Governors Center.

Elmore, R.F. (1991b). "Teaching, Learning, and Organization." Paper presented to the annual meeting of the American Eductional Research Association, San Francisco.

Elmore, R.F. (1992). "Why Restructuring Alone Won't Improve Teaching." *Educational Leadership* 49, 7: 44–48.

Englert, C.S., T.E. Raphael, L.M. Anderson, H.M. Anthony, and D.D. Stevens. (1991). "Making Strategies and Self-Talk Visible: Writing Instruction in Regular and Special Education Classrooms." *American Educational Research Journal* 28, 2: 337–372.

Finn, C. (1991). *We Must Take Charge: Our Schools and Our Future*. New York: Free Press.

Fullan, M.G. (1982). *The Meaning of Educational Change*. Toronto: Ontario Institute for Studies in Education.

Fullan, M.G. (1990). "Staff Development, Innovation, and Institutional Development." In *Changing School Culture Through Staff Development*, edited by B. Joyce. Alexandria, Va.: ASCD.

Fullan, M.G., B. Bennett, and C. Rolheiser-Bennett. (1990). "Linking Classroom and School Improvement." *Educational Leadership* 47, 8: 13–19.

Fullan, M.G., and M.B. Miles. (1991). "Getting Educational Reform Right: What Works, and What Doesn't." Article submitted to *Phi Delta Kappan*.

Fullan, M.G., and A. Pomfret. (1977). "Research on Curriculum and Instruction Implementation." *Review of Educational Research* 47, 1: 335–397.

Fullan, M.G., and S. Steigelbauer. (1991). *The New Meaning of Educational Change*. New York: Teachers College Press.

Gamoran, A., and M. Berends. (1987). "The Efforts of Stratification in Secondary Schools." *Review of Educational Research* 57, 4: 415–435.

Gardner, J.W. (1963). *Self-Renewal: The Individual and the Innovative Society*. New York: Harper and Row.

Gardner, J.W. (Winter 1987). "Self-Renewal." *National Forum*, 16–19.

Glass, G.V. (1982). "Meta-Analysis: An Approach to the Synthesis of Research Results." *Journal of Research in Science Teaching* 19, 2: 93–112.

Glickman, C.D. (1990). "Open Accountability for the '90s: Between the Pillars." *Educational Leadership* 47, 7: 38–42.

Glickman, C.D. (1993). *Renewing America's Schools: A Guide for School-Based Action*. San Francisco: Jossey-Bass.

Glickman, C.D., and L. Allen, eds. (1991). *Lessons from the Field: Renewing Schools Through Shared Governance and Action Research*. Athens, Ga.: Program for School Improvement, University of Georgia.

Goodlad, J. (1984). *A Place Called School*. New York: McGraw-Hill.

Goodlad, J., and F. Klein. (1970). *Looking Behind the Classroom Door*. Worthington, Ohio: Charles E. Jones.

Hall, G.E., and S.M. Hord. (1987). *Change in Schools: Facilitating the Process*. New York: State University of New York.

Hallinger, P., and C.E. McCary. (1991). "Using a Problem-Based Approach to Instructional Leadership Development." Paper prepared for presentation at the International Congress for School Effectiveness and Improvement, Cardiff, Wales.

Hargreaves, A., and R. Dowe. (1989). "Coaching as Unreflective Practice." Paper presented at the annual meeting of the American Educational Research Association, San Francisco.

Hawley, W.D., S. Rosenholtz, H.J. Goodstein, and T. Hasselbring. (1984). "Good Schools: What Research Says About Improving Student Achievement." *Peabody Journal of Education* 61, 4: 1–178.

Herzberg, F. (January-February 1968). "One More Time: How Do You Motivate Employees?" *Harvard Business Review* 5.

Hillock, G. (1987). "Synthesis of Research on Teaching Writing." *Educational Leadership* 44, 8: 71–82.

Hirsch, E.D. (1987). *Cultural Literacy: What Every American Needs to Know*. New York: Houghton Mifflin.

Holly, P. (1991). "Action Research Within Institutional Development: It's Becoming Second Nature to Us Now." Paper presented at the annual meeting of the American Educational Research Association, Chicago.

Hopkins, D. (1990). "Integrating Staff Development and School Improvement: A Study of Teacher Personality and School Climate." In *Changing School Culture Through Staff Development*, edited by B. Joyce. 1990 ASCD Yearbook. Alexandria, Va.: ASCD.

Hopkins, D. (1992) *School Improvement Through Assessment*. London: Carfax.

Hord, S.M., and G.E. Hall. (1982). *Procedure for Quantitative Analysis of Change Facilitator Intervention*. Austin: University of Texas Research and Development Center for Teacher Education.

Houle, C.O. (1980). *Continuing Learning in the Professions*. New York: Jossey-Bass.

Huberman, A.M. (1992). "Successful School Improvement: Reflections and Observations." *Successful School Improvement*. Critical introduction to M.G. Fullan. London: Open University Press.

Huberman, A.M., and M. Miles. (1984). *Innovation Up Close: How School Improvement Works*. New York: Plenum Press.

Huberman, A.M., and M.B. Miles. (1986). "Rethinking the Quest for School Improvement: Some Findings from the DESSI Study." In *Rethinking School Improvement: Research, Craft, and Concept*, edited by A. Lieberman. New York: Teachers College Press.

Jencks, C., et al. (1970). *Education Vouchers: A Report on Financing Elementary Education by Grants to Parents*. Cambridge, Mass.: Center for the Study of Public Policy.

Johnson, D.W., and R.T. Johnson. (1990). *Cooperation and Competition: Theory and Research*. Edina, Minn: Interaction Book Company.

Joyce, B., ed. (1977). *The Urban-Rural School Improvement Program*. Syracuse, N.Y.: Syracuse University, The Staff Development Dissemination Center.

Joyce, B. (1991). "Doors to School Improvement." *Educational Leadership* 48, 8: 59–62.

Joyce, B. (1992). "Cooperative Learning and Staff Development: Teaching the Method with the Method." *Cooperative Learning* 12, 2: 10–13.

Joyce, B., and E. Calhoun. (1991). "The New Meaning of Educational Change." *School Effectiveness and School Improvement* 2, 4: 336–343.

Joyce, B., C. Murphy, B. Showers, and J. Murphy. (1989). "Reconstructing the Workplace: School Renewal as Cultural Change." *Educational Leadership* 47, 3: 70–78.

Joyce, B., L. Peck, and C. Brown, eds. (1981). *Flexibility in Teaching*. White Plains, N.Y.: Longman, Inc.

Joyce, B., and B. Showers. (1988). *Student Achievement Through Staff Development*. White Plains, N.Y.: Longman.

Joyce, B., B. Showers, and M. Weil. (1992). *Models of Teaching*. 4th ed. Boston: Allyn and Bacon.

Lawrence, G. (1974). *Patterns of Effective Inservice Education: Review of Research*. Tallahassee: Florida State Department of Education.

Leithwood, K. (1990). "The Principal's Role in Teacher Development." In *Changing School Culture Through Staff Development*, edited by B. Joyce. 1990 ASCD Yearbook. Alexandria, Va.: ASCD.

Leithwood, K., and D. Montgomery. (1982). "The Role of the Elementary School Principal in Program Improvement." *Review of Educational Research* 52: 309–339.

Levin, M., and J.R. Levin. (1990). "Scientific Mnemonics: Methods for Maximizing More Than Memory." *American Educational Research Journal* 27, 2: 301–321.

Levine, D.U. (January 1991). "Creating Effective Schools: Findings and Implications from Research and Practice." *Phi Delta Kappan* 72, 5: 389–393.

Levine, D.U., and L.W. Lezotte. (1990). *Unusually Effective Schools: A Review and Analysis of Research and Practice*. Madison: University of Wisconsin, National Center for Effective Schools Research and Development.

Lewin, K. (1948). *Resolving Social Conflicts: Selected Papers on Group Dynamics*. New York: Harper and Row.

Lieberman, A., ed. (1988). *Building a Professional Culture in Schools*. New York: Teachers College Press.

Little, J.W. (1982). "Norms of Collegiality and Experimentation: Workplace Conditions of School Success." *American Educational Research Journal* 19, 3: 325–340.

Little, J.W. (1990). "The Persistence of Privacy: Autonomy and Initiative in Teachers' Professional Relations." *Teachers College Record* 91, 4: 509–536.

Lortie, D. (1975). *Schoolteacher*. Chicago: University of Chicago Press.

Loucks-Horsley, S., C.K. Harding, M.A. Arbuckle, L.B. Murray, C. Dubea, and M.K. Williams. (1987). *Continuing to Learn: A Guidebook for Teacher Development*. Andover, Mass.: The Regional Laboratory for Educational Improvement of the Northeast and Islands; and Oxford, Ohio: National Staff Development Council.

Louis, K.S., and M.B. Miles. (1990). *Improving the Urban High School*. New York: Teachers College Press.

Madden, N.A., R.E. Slavin, N.L. Karweit, L. Dolan, and B.A. Wasik. (1991). "Success for All." *Phi Delta Kappan* 72: 593–599.

Madden, N.A., R.E. Slavin, N.L. Karweit, L.J. Dolan, and B.A. Wasik. (1993). "Success for All: Longitudinal Effects of a Restructuring Program for Inner-City Elementary Schools." *American Educational Research Journal* 30, 1: 123–148.

Maeroff, G.I. (December 1991). "Assessing Alternative Assessment." *Phi Delta Kappan* 73, 4: 272–281.

Mann, D. (1989). "Conditional Deregulation." Paper presented at the annual meeting of the American Educational Research Association, San Francisco.

Marburger, C. (1989). *School-Based Improvement*. Columbia, Md.: National Committee for Citizens in Education.

McDonald, F. (1973). "Behavior Modification in Teacher Education." In *Behavior Modification in Education*, the 72nd Yearbook of NSSE, edited by H. Richey. Chicago: University of Chicago Press.

McLaughlin, M.W. (1990). "Rand Change Agent Study Revisited." *Educational Researcher* 19, 9: 11–15.

Miles, M.B. (1992). "40 Years of Change in Schools: Some Personal Reflections." Paper presented at the annual meeting of the American Educational Research Association, San Francisco.

Moore, D.R., and S. Davenport. (1989). *The New Improved Sorting Machine: Concerning School Choice*. Chicago: Designs for Change.

Mortimore, P., P. Sammons, L. Stoll, D. Lewis, and R. Ecob. (1988). *School Matters: The Junior Years*. London: Open Books.

Murphy, J. (1990). "The Educational Reform Movement of the 1980s: A Comprehensive Analysis." In *The Educational Reform Movement of the 1980s: Perspectives and Cases* (pp. 3–56), edited by J. Murphy. Newbury Park, Calif.: Corwin Press.

National Council of Teachers of Mathematics. (1989). *Curriculum and Evaluation Standards for School Mathematics*. Reston, Va.: NCTM.

National Council of Teachers of Mathematics. (1991). *Professional Standards for Teaching Mathematics*. Reston, Va.: NCTM.

Newmann, F.M. (1990). "Linking Restructuring to Authentic Student Achievement." Paper presented to the Indiana University Annual Education Conference, Bloomington.

Oakes, J. (1985). *Keeping Track: How Schools Structure Inequality*. New Haven: Yale University Press.

Oakes, J. (May 1992). "Can Tracking Research Inform Practice? Technical, Normative, and Political Considerations." *Educational Researcher* 21, 4: 12–21.

Oja, S.N., and L. Smulyan. (1989). *Collaborative Action Research: A Developmental Approach*. London: Falmer Press.

Owens, S., and D. Ranick. (1977). "The Greenville Program: A Commonsense Approach to Basics." *Phi Delta Kappan* 58: 531–533.

Pajak, E.F., and C.D. Glickman. (1989). "Dimensions of School District Improvement." *Educational Leadership* 46, 8: 61–64.

Phenix, P. (1964). *Realms of Meaning: A Philosophy of the Curriculum for General Education.* New York: McGraw-Hill.

Pink, W.T. (1989). "Effective Staff Development for Urban School Improvement." Paper presented at the annual meeting of the American Educational Research Association, San Francisco.

Potter, D.C., and M.E. Wall. (1992). "Higher Standards for Grade Promotion and Graduation: Unintended Effects of Reform." Paper presented at the annual meeting of the American Educational Research Association, San Francisco.

Pressley, M., J. Burkell, T. Cariglia-Bull, L. Lysynchuk, J.A. McGoldrick, B. Schneider, B.L. Snyder, S. Symons, and V.E. Woloshyn. (1990). *Cognitive Strategy Instruction That Really Improves Children's Academic Performance.* Cambridge: Brookline Books.

Pressley, M., and K.R. Harris. (1990). "What We Really Know About Strategy Instruction." *Educational Leadership* 48, 1: 31–34.

Pressley, M., J. Levin, and H. Delaney. (1982). "The Mnemonic Keyword Method." *Review of Educational Research* 52, 1: 61–92.

Rand Corporation. (1981). *A Study of Alternatives in American Education, Vol. 7: Conclusions and Policy Implications.* Santa Monica, Calif.: Author.

Raywid, M.A. (1985). "Family Choice Arrangements in Public Schools: A Review of the Literature." *Review of Educational Research* 55, 4: 435–467.

Raywid, M.A. (1987). "Public Choice, Yes; Vouchers, No!" *Phi Delta Kappan* 68, 10: 762–769.

Rolheiser-Bennett, C. (1986). *Four Models of Teaching: A Meta-Analysis of Student Outcomes.* Doctoral diss., University of Oregon, Eugene.

Rosenholtz, S. (1989). *Teachers' Workplace: The Social Organization of Schools.* White Plains, N.Y.: Longman.

Rutter, M., B. Maughan, P. Mortimore, J. Ouston, and A. Smith. (1979). *Fifteen Thousand Hours: Secondary Schools and Their Effects on Children.* Cambridge, Mass.: Harvard University Press.

Sadker, D., and M. Sadker. (1985). "Is the O.K. Classroom O.K.?" *Phi Delta Kappan* 66, 5: 358–361.

Sarason, S. (1982). *The Culture of the School and the Problem of Change.* 2nd ed. Boston: Allyn and Bacon.

Sarason, S. (1990). *The Predictable Failure of School Reform: Can We Change the Course Before It's Too Late?* San Francisco: Jossey-Bass.

Schaefer, R.J. (1967). *The School as a Center of Inquiry.* New York: Harper and Row.

Schön, D. (1982). *The Reflective Practitioner.* New York: Basic Books.

Sharan, S., and H. Shachar. (1988). *Language and Learning in the Cooperative Classroom.* New York: Springer-Verlag.

Sharan, S., ed. (1992). *Research on Cooperative Learning.* New York: Springer-Verlag.

Showers, B. (1989). "Implementation: Research-Based Training and Teaching Strategies and Their Effects on the Workplace and Instruction." Paper presented at the annual meeting of the American Educational Research Association, San Francisco.

Sirotnik, K.A. (1987). "Evaluation in the Ecology of Schooling." In *The Ecology of School Renewal: The Eighty-Sixth Yearbook of the National Society for the Study of Education*, edited by J.I. Goodlad. Chicago: The University of Chicago Press.

Sizer, T. (1984). *Horace's Compromise*. Boston: Houghton Mifflin.

Sizer, T.R. (1991). "No Pain, No Gain." *Educational Leadership* 48, 8: 32–34.

Sizer, T.R. (November 1992). "School Reform: What's Missing." *World Monitor* (The Christian Science Monitor Monthly), 20–27.

Slavin, R.E. (1987). "Ability Grouping and Student Achievement in Elementary Schools: A Best-Evidence Synthesis." *Review of Educational Research* 57, 293–336.

Slavin, R.E. (1990). "Achievement Effects of Ability Grouping in Secondary Schools: A Best-Evidence Synthesis." *Review of Educational Research* 60, 3: 471–500.

Slavin, R., N. Karweit, and B. Wasik. (1992). "Preventing Early School Failure." *Educational Leadership* 50, 4: 10–18.

Slavin, R.E., and N.A. Madden. (1989). "What Works for Students at Risk: A Research Synthesis." *Educational Leadership* 46, 5: 4–13.

Slavin, R.E., N.A. Madden, N. Karweit, B.J. Livermon, and L. Dolan. (1990). "Success for All: First-Year Outcomes of a Comprehensive Plan for Reforming Urban Education." *American Educational Research Journal* 27, 2: 255–278.

Sparks, G.M. (1983). "Synthesis of Research on Staff Development." *Educational Leadership* 41, 3: 65–72.

Spaulding, R. (1970). *Educational Intervention in Early Childhood*. Final Report for the Ford Foundation. Durham, N.C.: Ford Foundation.

Strusinski, M. (1989). "The Provision of Technical Support for School-Based Evaluations: The Researcher's Perspective." Paper presented at the annual meeting of the American Educational Research Association, San Francisco.

Sudderth, C. (1989). "The Social Battleground of School Improvement." Paper presented to the annual meeting of the American Educational Research Association, San Francisco.

Thelen, H. (1954). *Dynamics of Groups at Work*. Chicago: University of Chicago Press.

Timar, T. (1989). "The Politics of School Restructuring." *Phi Delta Kappan* 71, 4: 265–276.

Tye, K., ed. (1991). *Global Education: From Thought to Action*. 1991 ASCD Yearbook. Alexandria, Va.: ASCD.

Walberg, H.J. (1986). "What Works in a Nation Still at Risk." *Educational Leadership* 44, 1: 7–11.

Walberg, H.J. (1990). "Productive Teaching and Instruction: Assessing the Knowledge Base." *Phi Delta Kappan* 71, 6: 70–78.

Wallace, R.C., P.G. Lemahieu, and W.E. Bickel. (1990). "The Pittsburgh Experience: Achieving Commitment to Comprehensive Staff Development." *Changing School Culture Through Staff Development*, 1990 ASCD Yearbook, edited by B. Joyce. Alexandria, Va.: ASCD.

Waterman, R.H. (1988). *The Renewal Factor: How the Best Get and Keep the Competitive Edge*. New York: Bantam.

Weiss, C.H. (1990). "How Much Shared Leadership Is There in Public High Schools?" Paper presented at the annual meeting of the American Educational Research Association, Boston.

Whitford, B.L., P.C. Schlechty, and L.G. Shelor. (1987). "Sustaining Action Research Through Collaboration: Inquiries for Invention." *Peabody Journal of Education* 64, 3: 151–169.

Wiggins, G. (1989). "Teaching to the (Authentic) Test." *Educational Leadership* 46, 7: 41–47.

Wise, A. (1988). "The Two Conflicting Trends in School Reform: Legislated Learning Revisited." *Phi Delta Kappan* 69, 5: 328–333.

Wolf, J., and B. Joyce. (1992). "Just Read and Write." Materials presented at the annual meeting of the Association for Supervision and Curriculum Development, New Orleans.

Index

Current ASCD Networks

ASCD sponsors numerous networks that help members exchange ideas, share common interests, identify and solve problems, grow professionally, and establish collegial relationships. The following networks may be of particular interest to readers of this book:

Cooperative Learning
Harlan Rimmerman, Director, N. Kansas City Schl. Dist., 2000 N.E. 46th St., Kansas City, MO 64116; TEL (816) 453-5050

Educational Futurists
Barbara Vogl, Consultant, Change Mgmt. Systems, 5300 Glen Haven Rd., Soquel, CA 95073; TEL (408) 476-2905

Kathleen Maury, Mankato State Univ., 132 East Glencrest Dr., Mankato, MN 56001; TEL (507) 389-5704

High Schools Networking for Change
Gil James, Principal, Sprague High School, 2373 Kuebler Rd. South, Salem, OR 97302-9404; TEL (503) 399-3261, FAX (503) 399-3407

Learning Community
F. James Clatworthy, School of Education, Oakland Univ., Rochester, MI 48309-4401; TEL (313) 370-3052, FAX (313) 370-4202

Staff Development
Linda O'Neal, North East ISD, 10333 Broadway, Annex XI, San Antonio, TX 78217; TEL (210) 657-8652

Teacher Leadership
Ronnie Konner, West Essex Regional Schl. Dist., West Greenbrook Rd., N. Caldwell, NJ 07006; TEL (201) 228-1200, FAX (201) 575-7847

Understanding Educational Change
Michele Keenan, 407 Enos Place, Ho-Ho-Kus, NJ 07423; TEL (201) 612-0950, FAX (201) 670-3833

ASCD Networks Program Liaison
Agnes Crawford, Asst. Director, Field Services, Association for Supervision and Curriculum Development, 1250 N. Pitt St., Alexandria, VA 22314-1453; TEL (703) 549-9110, Ext. 506, FAX (703) 549-3891

Contact Network coordinators directly, or call the ASCD Networks Program Liaison, Agnes Crawford, at (703) 549-9110, Ext. 506.

We Want to Hear from You!

Please take a few minutes to answer a few questions about this book, *The Self-Renewing School*, by Bruce Joyce, James Wolf, and Emily Calhoun. Your responses will help the editors plan future ASCD publications.

1. Please rate this book on a scale of 1–10, with 10 being the highest positive score.

1	2	3	4	5	6	7	8	9	10

2. What is the primary reason you gave the book a high score?

3. What is the primary reason you gave the book a low score?

Please send your responses to: "Self-Renewing" Survey, ASCD Books, 1250 North Pitt Street, Alexandria, VA 22314-1453.

_____ For information about membership in the Association for Supervision and Curriculum Development (ASCD), check here and provide your name and address below.

_____ If you would like to receive an *ASCD Products Catalog*, check here, and provide your name and address.

Name _____

Title (or position) _____

Street Address _____

City/State/Zip _____

Daytime Phone (___) _____

Association for Supervision
and Curriculum Development
1250 North Pitt Street
Alexandria, VA 22314-1453
Telephone: (703) 549-9110
FAX: (703) 549-3891